Samuel Rutherford
of Anwoth

Samuel Rutherford of Anwoth

A Study in Pastoral Care

Bruce McLennan

Reformation Heritage Books
Grand Rapids, Michigan

Samuel Rutherford of Anwoth

Reformation Heritage Books
3070 29th St. SE
Grand Rapids, MI 49512
616–977–0889
orders@heritagebooks.org
www.heritagebooks.org

Printed in the United States of America
22 23 24 25 26 27/10 9 8 7 6 5 4 3 2 1

Library of Congress Cataloging-in-Publication Data

Names: McLennan, Bruce, author.
Title: Samuel Rutherford of Anwoth : a study in pastoral care / Bruce McLennan.
Description: Grand Rapids, Michigan : Reformation Heritage Books, [2022] | Includes bibliographical references.
Identifiers: LCCN 2022023981 (print) | LCCN 2022023982 (ebook) | ISBN 9781601789532 (paperback) | ISBN 9781601789549 (epub)
Subjects: LCSH: Rutherford, Samuel, 1600?-1661. | Presbyterian Church—Scotland—Clergy—Biography. | Scotland—Church history—17th century. | BISAC: RELIGION / Christian Church / History | RELIGION / Christian Ministry / Pastoral Resources
Classification: LCC BX9225.R94 M35 2022 (print) | LCC BX9225.R94 (ebook) | DDC 285.2411—dc23/eng/20220720
LC record available at https://lccn.loc.gov/2022023981

For additional Reformed literature, request a free book list from Reformation Heritage Books at the above regular or e-mail address.

Contents

Preface vii
Acknowledgments xiii

Part 1: The Life and Times of Samuel Rutherford

1. Church and Crown in Conflict 3
2. Two Contrasting Parts of Scotland 19
3. The Life of Samuel Rutherford 35
4. The Growth of a Soul 55

Part 2: The Pastoral Work of Samuel Rutherford

5. Key Emphases in Rutherford's Writings 73
6. Pastoral Advice to the Anwoth Flock 87
7. Reasoning with Souls, Making Salvation Sure 93
8. The Need for Sanctification and Mortification. 107
9. Counseling Some Who Had Doubts 113
10. Pastoral Concern for Children and Youth 119
11. Counsel to the Bereaved 127
12. Counseling the Dying 135

Conclusion 147

Appendix 1: The Source of Early Protestant Teachings in Aberdeen 157
Appendix 2: Coping with Minister Shortages during the Early Reformation 159
Glossary 161
Bibliography 163

Preface

This work is concerned, as the title indicates, with one particular aspect of the life and work of Samuel Rutherford—namely, as a shepherd of the Lord's people. He was much more than that, as can be seen from the attention now being given to other aspects of his religious involvement,[1] not to mention that he has been the subject of a number of university dissertations. Whether as a scholar in demand by universities in Scotland or Europe[2] or as a defender of the Reformed faith; as a political theorist or as a fierce debater on the principles of Presbyterian church government, especially during his time at the Westminster Assembly in London from 1643 to 1647, Rutherford was drawn into every aspect of the church life of Scotland.

---

1. Recent works include the following: Guy M. Richard, *The Supremacy of God in the Theology of Samuel Rutherford* (Milton Keynes, England: Paternoster, 2008); Matthew Vogan, ed., *Samuel Rutherford: An Introduction to His Theology*, Academic Series (Edinburgh: Scottish Reformation Society, 2012); and Matthew Vogan, ed., *"The King in His Beauty": The Piety of Samuel Rutherford* (Grand Rapids: Reformation Heritage Books, 2011).

2. In October 1639 Rutherford took up his position as professor of divinity in the New College (later St. Mary's College) of St. Andrews, to which was added principal of that college, then rector of the university in 1651. In addition, he was one of the ministers of the city along with Robert Blair. Not long after its founding in 1648, the University of Harderwyck in Holland invited him to become professor of divinity and Hebrew. A similar invitation came twice from the University of Utrecht in 1651. Rutherford declined all, "as he could not think of abandoning his own church in the perilous circumstances in which she then stood." Thomas Murray, *The Life of Samuel Rutherford* (Edinburgh: Oliphant and Sons, 1828), 248, 257–60.

A word that first came into English usage in the 1620s that may fittingly describe Samuel Rutherford is *polymath*, a master of many disciplines. He could perhaps be termed a religious polymath. While he was highly regarded by contemporaries for his contribution to various aspects of Scottish church life, Rutherford himself often made it abundantly clear that his first love, and that to which he believed he was clearly called, was preaching the gospel and shepherding the Lord's people. To fellow minister William Dalgleish he wrote from exile in Aberdeen, "I persuade you, my dear brother, that there is nothing out of heaven, next to Christ, dearer to me than my ministry."[3] After some introductory work in part 1, which will help set the scene, this vital aspect of his life and work will be the main emphasis in part 2.

Perhaps some comment on seventeenth-century spelling will be helpful. Spelling was not completely standardized in the early seventeenth century; therefore, names were spelled with slight differences. For example, the Christian name of Rutherford's first wife, Euphame, was also spelled Eupham and Euphan. The Aberdeen Dr. Baron is also spelled Barron. Anwoth was sometimes spelled Anworth. Even Rutherford's name has its variants: Rutherfoord, Rutherfoorde, Rutherfurd. Readers may well encounter several other variants.

By the early seventeenth century, Scottish preachers and writers were gradually leaving their native Scots behind and were beginning to express themselves more in English. Some works were edited by others much later than they were written, and editors altered the words to English. Where helpful, English words have been inserted in brackets, and this has been kept in this volume. Other works, for example Rutherford's letters, have been left as they were written, at least in the classic Bonar edition. Readers will encounter there some strange words or spellings. But those who wish to consult them will

3. Rutherford to William Dalgleish (letter 184), June 16, 1637, in *Letters of Samuel Rutherford*, ed. Andrew A. Bonar (London: Oliphants, 1891), 358. All subsequent quotations of Rutherford's letters will be from this edition.

be grateful for the sixteen-page glossary of terms at the end of that edition. There is also a glossary of terms at the end of this work.

Of the 365 extant letters Rutherford wrote, approximately 220 were penned during his "exile" in Aberdeen from the autumn of 1636 to the spring of 1638. A good number were written to the nobility of the land: for example, to Lords Boyd, Craighall, and Balmerino; to Lindsay of Byres and Lord Loudon; to the Earls of Lothian and Cassilis. One of Rutherford's reasons for writing to the nobility, which will be enlarged on later, was to enlist their support in defense of the Reformed faith, which he believed their predecessors had been instrumental in helping to establish.

Thirty-four letters were written to various members of the Gordon family of the Southwest, who exercised great influence for the gospel in that part of Scotland; eight, for example, were addressed to Alexander Gordon of Earlston, four to Robert Gordon of Knockbreck, and four to John Gordon of Cardoness, three to Cardoness, Younger. This in itself provides a striking contrast with the Northeast of Scotland, where the dominant family, the Catholic House of Gordon, was an obstacle to the Reformed faith and then championed episcopacy and the Royalist cause. This will be covered in chapter 2.

Rutherford also wrote to lairds, bailies, and provosts of towns. For example, to William Fullerton, provost of Kirkcudbright, he wrote from Aberdeen, encouraging him to continue to take a stand in opposition to Bishop Sydserff's attempt to imprison the eighty-year-old minister William Glendinning: "I earnestly entreat you to give your honour and authority to Christ, and for Christ: and be not dismayed for flesh and blood, while you are for the Lord, and for His truth and cause."[4]

He also wrote to soldiers and ministers of a strong Presbyterian persuasion like his own, and he wrote several most-touching letters to those experiencing bereavement.

One hundred seventy-one letters were written to women, which alone makes this a unique collection. His most regular

4. Rutherford to William Fullerton (letter 67), September 21, 1636, 146.

correspondents were women. Fifty-six letters were addressed to Lady (later Viscountess) Kenmure, who in 1628 had married John Gordon of Lochinvar. Rutherford frequently visited them in their nearby castle. Another early regular correspondent was Marion McNaught, wife of William Fullerton and niece to Gordon of Lochinvar. They lived a few miles from Anwoth, and Rutherford often visited their home. A close correspondent until her death in 1643, he wrote of her, "Blessed be the Lord! That in God's mercy I found in this country such a woman, to whom Jesus is dearer than her own heart, when there be so many that cast Christ over their shoulder."[5]

He wrote several letters to the wives of lairds and dignitaries, "that they might employ their female charms on their husbands in support of Presbyterianism. Sixty of the Aberdeen letters were addressed to ladies of social standing."[6]

There were a few letters written to the humbler sort—for example, Jean Brown, mother of the future minister and commentator John Brown of Wamphray; Jean Macmillan and Bethsaida Aird, parishioners; and Margaret Ballantyne, another likely parishioner. A small number have defied identification to this day.

Why were so few letters addressed to the humbler sort? Even bearing in mind Rutherford's reasons for writing to others, the answer may for the most part be accounted for by the illiteracy of rural Scotland in particular in those days. It has been estimated that "only ten to twenty percent of the rural population at that time could read."[7] This can be illustrated from that locality as follows. In addition to the Gordons and others who in 1639 signed "the humble petition of Galloway, to the Reverend Commission of Edinburgh" in an attempt to keep their beloved pastor at Anwoth, there were "172

5. Rutherford to John Kennedy (letter 22), February 2, 1632, 77.

6. Kingsley G. Rendell, *Samuel Rutherford: A New Biography of the Man and His Ministry* (Fearn, Ross-shire, Scotland: Christian Focus, 2003), 97.

7. Margo Todd, *The Culture of Protestantism in Early Modern Scotland* (New Haven, Conn.: Yale University Press, 2002), 25. "Judging by ability to sign, urban literacy as late as the 1630s hovered around 50 per cent, rural closer to 10–20 per cent for men; female literacy was less than ten per cent."

names of persons not able to write, but with their hand at the pen, assisted by James Gordon, Notary."[8] Compulsory elementary education was not introduced into Scottish schools until 1872, though the churches had done and continued to do what they could as the main educators at the local level. No doubt congregations would listen eagerly as John Gordon of Cardoness, Elder, as instructed, read to the congregation at Anwoth the two lengthy pastoral letters from Aberdeen, as would the saints at Kilmalcolm to the one reading his answers to the questions they had sent to him.

8. Murray, *Life of Samuel Rutherford*, 357.

Acknowledgments

I would like to acknowledge the cooperation and assistance of staff of the following centers in the production of this work: National Library of Scotland, Edinburgh; New College Library, University of Edinburgh; Dundee University Library; Dundee Central Public Library.

In days of restricted access to library facilities, online facilities have been particularly helpful. I am also especially grateful to the following: Still Waters Revival—Puritan Downloads; and the Evangelical Library, London (books by post).

For the final presentation of the work, I am deeply indebted to the editor, Mrs. Annette Gysen. Without her guidance and many suggestions for improvement, the work could not have reached its final state. She is to be commended for her great patience.

PART 1

The Life and Times of Samuel Rutherford

This part of the work sets the scene for our later study by opening up the salient features of the struggle for supremacy between the Crown and the Scottish Church in the late sixteenth and early seventeenth centuries. Attention is then given to the two areas where Rutherford spent his earliest adult years, drawing a contrast between them. A brief survey is then given of Rutherford's life against the backdrop of those areas. The scene is finally set by showing how Rutherford's exile in Aberdeen, in his own words, was the means of his further spiritual development.

1

Church and Crown in Conflict

The attitude of the Stuart kings toward the church in Scotland led inevitably to conflict in the sixteenth and seventeenth centuries. James VI of Scotland (1567–1603), later king of Great Britain (r. 1603–1625), was very proud of his kingcraft. Before he left Scotland, he had written, for the benefit of his young son and heir at that time Prince Henry (1594–1612), a work titled *Basilicon Doron*. In this work he put forward his theory of the divine right of kings, what today would more likely be called "absolute monarchy."[1] He put emphasis on his divine calling as a king. This contrasted with Protestant leaders like John Knox and Andrew Melville, ministers who had no doubt as to their own divine calling as preachers of the gospel.

In the conflict that emerged throughout James's reign, the church was at times in the ascendancy; at other times the king was. In April 1578 the Second Book of Discipline, a work largely of Andrew Melville, was given the church's approval. It proposed a church organization without bishops and superintendents. A general assembly with moderator, synods, and presbyteries would be the national framework. James VI, however, was determined to modify such a system, seeking to revive episcopacy in its place. In 1584 he persuaded the Scottish Parliament to pass the Black Acts, as they came to be called. These acts asserted the power of the king over all persons and estates, denounced "the new pretended presbyteries,"

1. J. H. S. Burleigh, *A Church History of Scotland* (London: Oxford University Press, 1973), 190.

and once again affirmed the authority of the bishops, who were to be responsible to the king, not the general assembly. James was reasserting his royal authority, both spiritual and temporal.[2]

In 1592, however, an act of Parliament was passed that has been called the Charter of Presbytery. It authorized "the government of the church under the assembly, by synods, presbyteries and kirk sessions." There was to be a general assembly that would meet once a year in the presence of the king or his commissioner at a time and place of the king's appointing.[3] James at once began to take advantage of this last point by choosing for the assembly to meet at places like Perth, Dundee, and Montrose, allowing ministers from the North, more sympathetic to the king, to attend.

Four years after the act was passed, there occurred the oft-mentioned encounter between Andrew Melville, the acknowledged leader of the Presbyterians, and the king in his royal palace of Falkland in Fife. Melville plucked James's sleeve, called him "God's sillie vassal," and reminded him quite forcefully as follows: "There are two kings and two kingdoms in Scotland. There is Christ Jesus the King and His kingdom the kirk, whose subject King James the Sixth is, and of whose kingdom not a king, not a lord, nor a head, but a member."[4]

Once enthroned in England in 1603, James postponed the annual meeting of the assembly. When nineteen ministers met in Aberdeen in defiance of this, they were condemned for treason; fourteen of them were imprisoned, and six eventually banished for life. Andrew Melville was put in the Tower of London, then banished from the realm, ending his days teaching at the University of Sedan. His nephew James, of a similarly strong Presbyterian stance, was sent up to Newcastle, never to be allowed to return to Scotland.[5] King

2. Gordon Donaldson, *Scotland: James V to James VII* (Edinburgh: Oliver and Boyd, 1965), 181, 198; and Burleigh, *Church History of Scotland*, 202.

3. Burleigh, *Church History of Scotland*, 204; and Donaldson, *Scotland: James V to James VII*, 199.

4. *The Diary of James Melville, 1556–1601*, ed. G. R. Kinloch (Edinburgh: Bannatyne Club 34, 1829), 370.

5. Donaldson, *Scotland: James V to James VII*, 204–5; and Burleigh, *Church History of Scotland*, 205–7.

James was getting rid of Presbyterian opposition to his desire for a church with bishops.

James further strengthened his control over the church by taking parliamentary action. In July 1606 an act "for the restitution of the estate of bishops" was passed. This act "stressed the importance of the episcopate as an essential part of the constitution of the kingdom."[6] In 1610, at a general assembly held in Glasgow, the church agreed to receive bishops as moderators of diocesan synods "with power to excommunicate offenders, ordain or depose ministers, and visit all churches within their diocese."[7]

Six years later the Court of High Commission was erected. It had the power to summon before it ministers who, if found guilty of offense, could be deposed or excommunicated, fined, or imprisoned. The following year, 1617, saw James's only return visit to Scotland. Under his instructions the Chapel Royal at Holyrood in Edinburgh was made to resemble a place of Anglican worship. The complaint of the people was, "First came the organs, now the images, and ere long we shall have the mass."[8]

James began the process of liturgical revision in 1601 and abandoned it in 1621. It was later revived by Charles I in 1629.[9] Donaldson points out that James's definite pursuit of liturgical changes had begun in 1614. First, it was a royal proclamation ordering that Holy Communion should be celebrated at Easter. The following year the University of St. Andrews was instructed to observe the greater festivals of the Christian year. All colleges were to use the Book of Common Prayer for parts of their services.[10] Both ministers and bishops were very much against any further liturgical changes.

---

6. Donaldson, *Scotland: James V to James VII*, 205.

7. Thomas McCrie, *Sketches of Scottish Church History: Embracing the Period from the Reformation to the Revolution* (Edinburgh: John Johnstone, 1841), 159.

8. McCrie, *Sketches of Scottish Church History*, 161.

9. Gordon Donaldson, *The Making of the Scottish Prayer Book of 1637* (Edinburgh: Edinburgh University Press, 1954), 31, 41.

10. Donaldson, *Scotland: James V to James VII*, 208.

Nevertheless, in 1618, what came to be called the Five Articles of Perth was passed by a compliant general assembly. These stipulated the following: kneeling at Communion; allowing Communion to be given privately to the sick; administering baptism in private houses as required; presenting children of eight years to the bishop for confirmation; and commemorating the birth, passion, resurrection, and ascension of the Lord Jesus Christ and the descent of the Holy Spirit at Pentecost on set occasions. Many ministers and congregations did not take the introduction of these articles very seriously nor were the bishops too eager to enforce them, fearing the likely opposition to their introduction. Indeed, the first three of them, in particular, were contrary to the then-current practice of Reformed churches.[11] Samuel Rutherford denounced these articles repeatedly in his letters not only to his parishioners but also to various other correspondents in the 1630s.

Matters Come to a Head under Charles I

James sought to advance episcopacy in order to strengthen his royal power. With his son, who succeeded him as Charles I in 1625, it was more than that. It was a matter of conscience. To Charles, a church that did not have bishops was not a proper church. It was not until 1633 that Charles belatedly came north for his coronation. With him was his queen, Henrietta Maria, daughter of Henry IV of France. A practicing Roman Catholic, she was surrounded by her Romanist chaplains, who were in constant attendance. She was known to exercise great influence over the king.

With Charles also was William Laud, soon to become archbishop of Canterbury. He was the king's chief adviser in ecclesiastical matters. Donaldson records that "on that visit he ordered the use of the English Prayer Book in certain places, and his coronation, in the abbey church of Holyrood, was conducted with a splendour of ornament and vesture unfamiliar in Scotland."[12]

11. Burleigh, *Church History of Scotland*, 208.
12. Donaldson, *Scotland: James V to James VII*, 306.

The following year, 1636, a code of canons, or rules for the church, was published, every minister being obliged to accept it.[13] It incorporated the Five Articles of Perth and required acceptance of a liturgy that appeared the following year. While it made some concessions to Scottish prejudice, there was much that was unacceptable about it: "the turning of the table altarwise, and most commonly calling it an altar" and forbidding extempore prayers. In spite of the Scots' objection to observing the Christian year, they were presented with a prayer book that increased the number of saints' days, giving Scotland twenty-nine to England's twenty-seven.[14]

To many people, this new liturgy, dubbed "Laud's liturgy," smacked of popery. It was actually, however, the Scottish bishops, and not Laud, who were responsible for "the chief characteristics of the book of 1637" and for its printing.[15] What also rankled with many Scots was the manner in which it was introduced from England without any consultation with the people. In his sermon "The Apostle's Choice" (Phil. 3:7–8), preached at St. Andrews, Rutherford put the matter plainly: "What is the quarrel that the prelates and their adherents have at Scotland this day? It is not because we will not follow the Bible and God's ordinances in His worship; but their quarrel at us is, because we will not follow a service book and ceremonies, and because we will not have a creature of their upsetting, a prelate, to be the head of the Church."[16]

It was at this point that Lord Loudon, who shortly after was to play an important role at the signing of the National Covenant in February and March 1638, gave what ought to have been a timely warning. He told Charles I, "Sire, the people of Scotland will obey you in everything with the utmost cheerfulness, provided you do

---

13. The full title of the canons was "Canons and Constitutions Ecclesiastical, gathered and put in form for the Government of the Church of Scotland, ratified and approved by His Majesty's royal warrant, and ordained to be observed by the clergy and all others whom they concern." Burleigh, *Church History of Scotland*, 213.

14. Donaldson, *Making of the Scottish Prayer Book*, 74–75.

15. Donaldson, *Making of the Scottish Prayer Book*, 78–79.

16. Samuel Rutherford, *Quaint Sermons Hitherto Unpublished*, ed. A. A. Bonar (London: Hodder and Stoughton, 1885), 354.

not touch their religion and conscience."[17] Charles did not heed this warning. The day set for the introduction of the prayer book was July 23, 1637.

At this time many of the godly Presbyterian ministers were exerting their influence with the nobility and other leading figures, seeking to enlist their support to prevent this innovation. Rutherford was at the fore of this. He wrote three letters to the aforementioned Lord Loudon (John Campbell, first Earl of Loudon, son of Sir James Campbell of Lawers). In the first of them, he was critical of the tendency of some nobles to "slip from Christ's cause as they do, and stand looking on with their hands folded behind their back when louns [rogues, worthless fellows] are running with the spoil of Zion on their back." He continued, "It were the glory and honour of you, who are the nobles of this land, to plead for your wronged Bridegroom and His oppressed spouse, as far as zeal and standing law will go with you."[18]

Loudon had obviously responded to Rutherford's urgings, for in a second letter he wrote thus: "I rejoice exceedingly to hear that your Lordship hath a good mind to Christ, and His now borne-down truth. My very dear Lord, go on, in the strength of the Lord, to carry your honours and worldly glory to the New Jerusalem. For this cause your Lordship received these of the Lord. This is a sure way for the establishment of your house, if ye be of those who are willing, in your place, to build Zion's old waste places in Scotland."[19]

Early in January 1638, Rutherford wrote again, beseeching Loudon to go on "as ye have worthily begun, in purging of the Lord's house in this land, and plucking down the sticks of Antichrist's filthy nest, this wretched Prelacy." He pointed out that the eyes of "many noble, many holy, many learned and worthy ones, in our neighbourhood churches about, are upon you."[20]

Rutherford wrote to several other nobles and lairds: Lord Boyd, Lord Craighall, and Lord Lindsay, and the Earl of Cassilis. To the Earl

17. McCrie, *Sketches of Scottish Church History*, 202.
18. Rutherford to Lord Loudon (letter 116), March 9, 1637, 235.
19. Rutherford to Lord Loudon (letter 258), September 10, 1637, 504–5.
20. Rutherford to Lord Loudon (letter 281), January 1, 1638, 543–45.

of Cassilis he wrote, reminding him of how his honorable ancestors "with the hazard of their lives, brought Christ to our land." He urged him on to action as one of Zion's friends: "It is no wisdom (howbeit it be the state-wisdom now in request) to be silent, when they are casting lots for a better thing than Christ's coat.... O my dear and noble Lord, go on (howbeit the wind be in your face) to back our princely Captain. Be courageous for Him.... Now while this piece of the afternoon of your day is before you...let your worldly glory, honour, and might be for our Lord Jesus."[21] To John Osburn, provost of Ayr, he wrote, "Serve Christ. Back Him; let His cause be your cause; give not an hair-breadth of truth away; for it is not yours, but God's."[22] To the Laird of Gaitgairth Rutherford wrote appreciatively of his stance for the Lord: "I bless the Lord, who hath graced you to own Christ now, when so many are afraid to profess Him, and hide Him, for fear they suffer loss by avouching Him.... Worthy and much honoured Sir, go on to own Christ, and His oppressed truth."[23]

The Second Reformation

The furor that took place in St. Giles, Edinburgh, when Dean Hanna began to read the new liturgical service led to the dean and the bishop of Edinburgh being ushered to safety to avoid mob violence. Donaldson regards this incident as stage-managed: "The riot in the church of St. Giles on 23 July 1637 was not a spontaneous outbreak, but the chosen occasion for a demonstration by a powerful opposition which was already organized into something little short of conspiracy."[24] Petitions for the removal of the liturgy deluged the Edinburgh council, and crowds of people from Fife and the Lothians gathered in Edinburgh. King Charles's response was simply to order the dispersal of the petitioners. Following this were meetings and organizing petitions in which noblemen, barons, burgesses, and ministers took part. A second riot took place in Edinburgh, directed

21. Rutherford to Earl of Cassilis (letter 268), September 9, 1637, 520–21.
22. Rutherford to John Osburn (letter 149), March 14, 1637, 280.
23. Rutherford to Laird of Gaitgairth (letter 237), September 7, 1637, 472.
24. Donaldson, *Making of the Scottish Prayer Book*, 83.

against Lord Treasurer Traquair, the bishop of Galloway, and the magistrates of Edinburgh. When Traquair sought to explain matters to the king, Charles remained unyielding.

The next stage was drawing up the National Covenant. The term *Second Reformation* is given to the period from the signing of the National Covenant to the accession of Charles II, when episcopacy was restored. In the sixteenth and seventeenth centuries, there were many religious covenants, or bonds, as many as thirty-one being drawn up between 1556 and 1683. Some involved only a few individuals, towns, or parishes. The National Covenant, as its name indicates, was embraced by the whole country, with the exception of the town of Aberdeen and the surrounding country and parts of the Highlands. It was drawn up by Alexander Henderson, minister of Leuchars, and Archibald Johnston of Wariston, a young lawyer with strong Puritan principles. It was revised by Lords Rothes, Loudon, and Balmerino. It was signed on February 28, 1638, in the Greyfriars' Church, Edinburgh, by leading nobles and barons, then on March 1 by ministers and burgesses and also many lawyers.

It was decided that a copy should be given to every town and parish and that the universities should be "pressed" to sign. Those who signed promised to uphold the Reformed church and the true religion.[25] Donaldson comments, "It was an ingenious stroke to begin with a recital of the old anti-popish covenant of 1581, which King James had signed.... Here was something more than anti-popery, for this was an appeal to the rule of law, against the royal prerogative and the king's arbitrary courses, an appeal to history and to precedent. Here, too, was an assertion of parliamentary authority, for the list of statutes implied that parliament made the laws and that only parliament could change the laws."[26] All those who signed were indicating total disregard of all changes the king would make until they had been considered in free assemblies and by Parliament.

25. Burleigh, *Church History of Scotland*, 218.

26. Donaldson, *Scotland: James V to James VII*, 313–14.

There followed later that year, in November and December, the first free general assembly to meet in twenty years. It met in the High Kirk of Glasgow. This assembly, the elections for which were controlled by the Covenanters, annulled the detested canons, the liturgy, and the Five Articles and abolished the High Commission and deposed the bishops. The assembly continued to meet, even after the king's commissioner, the Marquis of Hamilton, dissolved it in Charles I's name, proclaiming its continued sitting as treasonable.[27]

As far as King Charles was concerned, the Covenanters were now rebels, for he could never abandon his twin beliefs in divine right monarchy and divine right episcopacy. They must be dealt with by force of arms. What followed was called the Bishops' Wars. But because of lack of funds, lack of support for a war among his own subjects, and lack of experienced commanders, Charles had to agree to a truce before any serious fighting had taken place. The First Bishops' War, therefore, ended with the Pacification of Berwick in 1639, with Charles agreeing to appoint an assembly to meet in Edinburgh followed by a parliament. Charles, however, also appealed to the English Parliament to finance the Second Bishops' War. This brought the Scots into England. They occupied Newcastle and Durham. After a defeat at Newburn in August 1641, Charles was forced to rely on the help of what came to be known as the Long Parliament to ratify the Treaty of London in August 1641.[28]

This Long Parliament, so called because it met from 1640 to 1660, was strongly Puritan and Presbyterian in its sympathies and was concerned to get rid of the English episcopate. When Charles raised his standard at Nottingham in August 1642, the English Civil War had begun. What brought the Scots into the war was the English parliamentary party's need for help. This was granted once the English Parliament gave its signature to what came to be known as the Solemn League and Covenant (1643).

---

27. Burleigh, *Church History of Scotland*, 220–21.
28. Burleigh, *Church History of Scotland*, 222.

The English Parliament wanted a reformation of the doctrine, worship, and government of the Church of England. The Solemn League and Covenant was a religious bond pledging that the two countries would get rid of episcopacy in England and popery in Ireland. Very ambitiously, it intended to bring the churches of the three kingdoms under one king, "to the nearer conjunction and uniformity in Religion, Confession of Faith, Form of Church Government, Directory for worship and Catechising...according to the Word of God and the example of the best Reformed Churches."[29] There was, however, a fundamental difference of intent between the two countries. As Robert Baillie, minister of Kilwinning, put it, "The English were for a civil League, we for a religious Covenant."[30]

What did result was setting up the Westminster Assembly, which began meeting on July 1, 1643, as a sort of parliamentary advisory commission. The great majority of those in attendance were Presbyterian in sympathy, though there were five Independents present. The Anglicans did not attend. An invitation was sent to the general assembly of the Church of Scotland to send representatives. Accordingly, Alexander Henderson, Robert Baillie, Samuel Rutherford, and George Gillespie went south to London, together with three ruling elders, the Earl of Cassilis, Lord Maitland, and Johnston of Wariston. Though they had no voting rights, they vigorously defended in debate the Presbyterian form of church government, "exercising an influence out of all proportion to their numbers."[31] To fellow minister Thomas Wylie of Borgue in the stewartry of Kirkcudbright, Rutherford wrote,

> I am now called for to England; the government of the Lord's house in England and Ireland is to be handled. My heart beareth me witness, and the Lord who is greater knoweth, my faith was never prouder than to be a common rough country barrowman in Anwoth; and that I could not look at

29. Burleigh, *Church History of Scotland*, 225.

30. *The Letters and Journals of Robert Baillie*, ed. David Laing (Edinburgh: Bannatyne Club 73, 1841–1842), 2:90.

31. John Coffey, *Politics, Religion, and the British Revolutions: The Mind of Samuel Rutherford* (Cambridge, England: Cambridge University Press, 1997), 52.

> the honour of being a mason to lay the foundation for many generations, and to build the waste places of Zion in another kingdom, or to have a hand or finger in that carved work in the cedar and almug trees in that new temple.[32]

Over a period of four years, the following were produced. First, the Directory for the Public Worship of God was intended to replace the English prayer book. This was followed by the Confession of Faith and the Shorter and Larger Catechisms. These documents have stood the test of time, being used in Reformed churches throughout the English-speaking world.[33]

The Covenanters Divide

Although the National Covenant had received a good measure of support throughout most of Scotland, by the late 1640s divisions among the Covenanters themselves began to appear. The Civil War had not gone well for King Charles, who for a time was in the Scottish camp. The English army was composed largely of those of Independent church persuasion and was growing in power. Establishing presbyterianism in England was now a remote possibility. These facts, together with concern over the likely fate of the king in English hands, led to three Scottish nobles, Loudon, Lanark, and Lauderdale, entering into an agreement with Charles, known as the Engagement, on December 26–27, 1647. By this, the Scots offered to help restore Charles peacefully to freedom and authority, if necessary by force of arms. For his part, Charles agreed to confirm the Solemn League and Covenant and establish Presbyterian government and worship in England for three years. Charles also agreed to cooperate with the Westminster divines to arrive at an ecclesiastical settlement and to suppress heretics and schismatics. The nobles behind the Engagement hoped that this would bring all parties together in support of the king.[34]

---

32. Rutherford to Thomas Wylie (letter 306), October 20, 1643, 615.
33. Burleigh, *Church History of Scotland*, 225–26.
34. Donaldson, *Scotland: James V to James VII*, 336–37; and Burleigh, *Church History of Scotland*, 229.

What it actually did, tragically, was divide the Covenanters into two groups. Following the Engagement and a military campaign into England at the general assembly of the church in July 1648, the Engagement was condemned. Then on January 23, 1649, the Scottish Parliament passed the Act of Classes. By this, those who were involved in the Engagement were to be excluded from public offices and the army, being classed as "malignants." The following year, however, in light of the present invasion of Cromwell from England (for the Scots had declared the king's son to be Charles II, which was as good as a declaration of war), the Scottish Parliament removed much of the legislation of the Act of Classes, allowing more people to fight in the army.

In December 1650 they passed the Public Resolutions to permit this. The general assembly approved of this. Those who supported the Public Resolutions were known as Resolutioners. Approximately 750 of the 900 ministers were of the Resolutioner persuasion. Those who objected to the haste with which arrangements for Charles's coronation were proceeding, even though he had given no evidence of a change in his principles, were very much in the minority.[35] They were known as Protesters. On the Resolutioner side were men like David Dickson, Robert Baillie, and George Hutcheson; in the ranks of the Protesters were such as Samuel Rutherford, James Guthrie, and Patrick Gillespie. In the midst of the Resolutioner and Protester dispute, there were those who sought to mediate. A conference that would bring the two groups together was arranged to meet at Edinburgh on June 1, 1655. Only a few ministers attended. They met in conference again in November that year, but after a few months, "the enmity was more bitter than before."[36]

James Durham, minister of the Inner High Church, Glasgow, being deeply troubled by the division in the church, penned what has been called his *Dying Testament*. So weak was he that he had to dictate

---

35. Donaldson, *Scotland: James V to James VII*, 353.

36. *Diary of Sir Archibald Johnston of Wariston*, vol. 3, *1655–1660*, ed. James D. Ogilvie, Scottish History Society 3 (Edinburgh: Edinburgh University Press and A. Constable Ltd., 1940), ix, xiv–xvi.

the fourth part, which had the situation of the Scottish Presbyterian church very much in mind. This work, with the rather forbidding title *A Treatise concerning Scandal*, was a sincere attempt to reconcile the two parties. He pleaded for "mutual condescending." On both sides, "one party should not expect full submission from the other, for that is not union, but dominion."[37] Ministers should be aware of how dreadful such a division was in the eyes of God, how it would cause the flock to stumble.[38] He pleaded for tenderness and respect for others' opinions.[39] He pointed to the example of the apostle Paul, who repeatedly laid a stress on unity in his epistles.[40] Durham went as far, in the hope of reconciliation, as to say that where there was a division into a greater and smaller number, "and the greater will not be induced to remove their determination, it is no way sinful to the lesser to join with them notwithstanding, they having their own freedom and liberty cautioned."[41] He concluded his pleading with these words: "Does not bitterness grow to an height among orthodox men, as if each of them were enemies to the truth of Christ, and enemies to one another's persons?… And shall, alas! Shall the weight of all these sad and religion ruining consequences be stated upon the refusing of such condescendence as is here called for? God forbid."[42]

What was tragic about this situation was that the dispute was not over doctrinal differences nor was there any question of heresy. This peaceable admonition, for all that it has become a classic in its genre, failed in its purpose for two reasons. First, it came too late, being only published in 1659. By this time there were rival assemblies (until banned in 1653), rival presbyteries, and even rival ministers in the same parish. Second, it meant that long-standing friends and colleagues were separated, often for their lifetime. This division

37. James Durham, *The Dying Man's Testament to the Church of Scotland, or A Treatise concerning Scandal* (Dallas, Tex.: Naphtali Press, 1990), 269–70.

38. Durham, *Dying Man's Testament*, 278–79.

39. Durham, *Dying Man's Testament*, 281.

40. Durham, *Dying Man's Testament*, 285.

41. Durham, *Dying Man's Testament*, 323.

42. Durham, *Dying Man's Testament*, 358.

continued when the persecution of the 1660s began.[43] Indeed, looking back on those years more than two centuries later, James Walker had this to say of the Resolutioner-Protester controversy:

> It put ill blood into our Church life, which a century and a half did not expel. What might have come of it had the Church been free of the Commonwealth disabilities, it is impossible to say. When the days of suffering came, you might have expected an end to divisions, and a union of heart and effort against the common enemy. But, as you know, it was far otherwise. Bitter variances—growing even more bitter—arose. The persecutor, with his indulgences, threw in an apple of discord among those noble witnesses of Christ, and they took to fighting in the furnace.[44]

The Commonwealth government treated Scotland as a conquered country, which required an occupying force of thirty-six thousand men and five forts at Leith, Inverness, Inverlochy, Perth, and Ayr, with lesser forts in more remote parts of the country. General George Monck and eight commissioners "of the parliament of England for ordering and managing the affairs of Scotland" initially managed the affairs of the country. From October 1651 on, England and Scotland were meant to be one commonwealth, with Scottish delegates to be sent to London. Few Scots, however, ever sat in the Westminster Parliament.[45]

With regard to church matters, the religious life of Scotland could not but suffer some harm from a church divided. The Cromwellian government, however, was concerned that the preaching of the gospel by faithful ministers should continue unabated. While this was welcomed, what both Resolutioners and Protesters found difficult to accept was the Cromwellian toleration of all other church groups, prelatists and papists excepted. While they were united in

---

43. J. King Hewison, *The Covenanters* (Glasgow: John Smith and Son, 1908), 1:452.

44. James Walker, *The Theology and Theologians of Scotland Chiefly of the Seventeenth and Eighteenth Centuries* (Edinburgh: T&T Clark, 1888), 104–5.

45. Donaldson, *Scotland: James V to James VII*, 346–47.

their opposition to "sectaries," relations between Resolutioners and Protesters grew more and more bitter.[46]

As to the religious life of the nation in those troubled times, evidence suggests a decline in spiritual conditions. One observer from south of the border deplored what he saw as follows:

> Instead of having no God but one, the generality of people… do idolise and set up their ministers…. All must fall down before this golden calf and submit to this government…. I have not known any of them to spend [the Lord's Day] in religious exercises, only in a bare cessation from labour and work…, spending their time in laziness and vanity…. Whoredom and fornication is the common darling sin of the nation.[47]

The general assembly issued a "solemn and seasonable warning" as to the nation's sinful state.[48] Several kirk session records indicate an increase in all kinds of sin.[49] In the capital city of Edinburgh, the spiritual state of congregations was so bad in the eyes of ministers that no Communion was celebrated between 1648 and 1655.[50]

Samuel Rutherford's life span coincided not only with the conflict between church and Crown but also with more than a decade of division in the church and with warfare, which had taken its toll on the nation. Commenting on the decline in the 1650s, Burleigh summed it up thus: "The Covenanting movement which began as almost a national movement thus broke down in dissension and strife."[51]

---

46. Burleigh, *Church History of Scotland*, 231.

47. Samuel Rawson Gardiner, ed., *Letters and Papers Illustrating the Relations between Charles II and Scotland in 1650*, vol. 17 of Publications of the Scottish History Society (Edinburgh: Edinburgh University Press, 1894), 137–39.

48. Alexander Peterkin, ed., *Records of the Kirk of Scotland, Containing the Acts and Proceedings of the General Assemblies, from 1638 Downwards* (Edinburgh: John Sutherland, 1838), 423–27.

49. Robert Chambers, *Domestic Annals of Scotland, from the Reformation, to the Rebellion of 1745* (Edinburgh: W. and R. Chambers, 1861), 2:198.

50. Donaldson, *Scotland: James V to James VII*, 354.

51. Burleigh, *Church History of Scotland*, 232.

2

Two Contrasting Parts of Scotland

This chapter looks at two somewhat contrasting parts of early seventeenth-century Scotland where Samuel Rutherford resided for part of his life. Although the Reformed faith was established in both of these areas, as in other parts of Scotland, by the early seventeenth century the contrast in these two areas was more marked.

The Southwest of Scotland

The reforming tradition in this part of the country went back to at least the early sixteenth century, when Alexander Gordon of Airds, in the stewartry of Kirkcudbright, sheltered some of the followers of John Wycliffe and read selections of his writings to his neighbors from the shelter of wooded areas on his estate. It was the New Testament in the "vulgar tongue."[1] With regard to Ayrshire, M. H. B. Sanderson has commented that "interest in the vernacular scriptures, anti-clerical attitudes and iconoclastic activity, all of which characterized the lay reform movement in Ayrshire at an early stage, reflect its lollard origins."[2]

Another early Protestant in the Southwest was Alexander Stewart, eldest son of Stewart of Garlies. He preached the Reformed faith in Dumfries and its districts. When the first general assembly met in 1560, Stewart was a commissioner from the kirks of Nithsdale.

---

1. A. S. Morton, *Galloway and the Covenanters; or, The Struggle for Religious Liberty in the South-West of Scotland* (Paisley, Scotland: Alexander Gardener, 1914), 26.

2. M. H. B. Sanderson, *Ayrshire and the Reformation: People and Change* (East Linton, Scotland: Tuckwell Press, 1997), 42.

Other family names regularly associated with the defense of the Reformed faith include Lord Cassilis, Lord Glencairn, and his son Lord Kilmaurs.[3]

At the Reformation Parliament, which met in Edinburgh on August 1, 17, and 24, 1560, twenty-two men from Ayrshire of a variety of ranks and stations were present in support of reform.[4] The first year for which there are full details of the staff of the Reformed church in Galloway is 1563. There were seven or eight ministers, six exhorters, and twenty-five readers (see appendix 2), which makes a total of nearly forty Reformed clergy for the forty-five parishes of Galloway. This had increased to around fifty by 1574. Of these, about three-fifths of the Galloway readers had been either priests or monks. Gordon Donaldson comments, "The figures for 1563 amply demonstrate that continuity in personnel was a conspicuous feature of the Reformation in Galloway."[5]

The son-in-law of John Knox, John Welsh (or Welch), a man given to much prayer,[6] was for a few years minister at Kirkcudbright in the late 1580s. While there, he "reaped a harvest of converts there which subsisted long after his departure, and were a part of Mr. Samuel Rutherford's flock, while he was minister at Anwoth."[7]

Welsh moved to Ayr in 1590, where he experienced a part of the Southwest sadly in need of a gospel ministry. The spiritual state of the town and surrounding country is described by John Howie:

---

3. Morton, *Galloway and the Covenanters*, 26–27.

4. Sanderson, *Ayrshire and the Reformation*, 105.

5. Gordon Donaldson, "The Galloway Clergy at the Reformation," *Dumfriesshire and Galloway Natural History and Antiquarian Society Transactions* 30, ser. 3 (1951–1952): 48. Donaldson points out also (p. 50) that the Roman Catholic clergy produced few ministers but did produce readers and exhorters, suggesting that the quality of the old church clergy was not very high.

6. Robert Fleming noted "that of every twenty-four hours, he gave usually eight to prayer, if other necessary and urgent duties did not hinder, yea, spent many days and nights, which he set apart in fasting and prayer, for the condition of the church." Robert Fleming, *The Fulfilling of the Scripture* (London: Forgotten Books, 2018), 1:361.

7. John Gillies, *Historical Collections of Accounts of Revival* (Edinburgh: Banner of Truth, 1981), 167.

"When he came first to the town, the country was so wicked and the hatred of godliness so great, that there could not be found one in all the town who would let him a house to dwell in, so he was constrained to accommodate himself for a time.... The place was so divided into factions, and filled with bloody conflicts, that a man could hardly walk the streets with safety."[8]

At Ayr he preached every day, studied with great diligence, and also spent a third part of his time in prayer. After a while, Ayr became a peaceable town. More than that, "in respect of spiritual fruit, he was highly successful. David Dickson, who was afterward minister of Irvine and had great encouragement in his own ministry there, used to say that the gleaning of the grapes of Ayr in Welch's time was equal to the vintage of Irvine."[9]

Imprisoned for a time in Blackness Castle for meeting with the general assembly at Aberdeen in 1605 against the king's wishes, Welsh wrote a letter to the Countess of Wigtown. In it he declared himself willing to suffer martyrdom for maintaining that Christ was the Head of the church, which was free in its government from all other jurisdiction but Christ's.[10]

When the general assembly met at Perth in 1618, those present from Galloway who opposed bringing in innovations in the form of the Five Articles were the ministers of Tongland, Glenluce, and Leswalt. The commissioner for Kirkcudbright likewise voted against the articles.[11]

It was in 1618 that David Dickson was ordained minister at Irvine, having previously been regent at Glasgow University where, together with Robert Blair and Robert Boyd, he had been training young men for the ministry of the word. He remained twenty-three

---

8. John Howie, *The Scots Worthies*, rev. W. H. Carslaw (Edinburgh: Oliphant, Anderson and Ferrier, 1870), 121–22.

9. W. G. Blaikie, *The Preachers of Scotland from the Sixth to the Nineteenth Century* (Edinburgh: Banner of Truth, 2001), 85–86.

10. W. K. Tweedie, ed., *Scottish Puritans: Select Biographies* (Edinburgh: Banner of Truth, 2008), 1:23.

11. Morton, *Galloway and the Covenanters*, 60.

years in Irvine, apart from a brief banishment to Turriff in Aberdeenshire for his opposition to the Perth Articles. Irvine, in fact, became a beacon of gospel light in that part of Scotland: "People under exercise and soul-concern came from every place about Irvine and attended on his sermons, and the most eminent and serious Christians from all corners of the Church came and joined him at his communions, which were indeed times of refreshing from the presence of the Lord; yea, not a few came from distant places and settled at Irvine, that they might be under the drop of his ministry."[12]

A wonderful awakening took place in 1625 in the parish of Stewarton and beyond in which Dickson played a major role. Robert Fleming (1630–1694), minister first at Cambuslang and then, after the Restoration of Charles II, in the Scots congregation at Rotterdam, describes what took place:

> A very solemn and extraordinary out-letting of the Spirit… whilst the persecution of the church there was hot from the prelatic party; this by the profane rabble of that time was called the Stewarton-sickness, for in that parish first, but after through much of that country, particularly at Irvine, under the famous Mr. Dickson, it was most remarkable, where it can be said… that for a considerable time, few Sabbaths did pass, without some evidently converted, and some convincing proofs of the power of God accompanying his word.[13]

This revival spread from house to house until it covered a good part of the valley in Ayrshire through which the River Stewarton flows. Robert Wodrow summed it up by saying, "It had a marvellous effect and served as an antidote to the prelatising influences of the time, *which tended to exalt the authority of the Church to the ignoring of personal piety*."[14]

---

12. Gillies, *Historical Collections of Accounts of Revival*, 182.

13. Robert Fleming, *The Fulfilling of the Scripture* (1801; repr., London: Forgotten Books, 2018), 1:354–55.

14. Tweedie, *Scottish Puritans*, 1:316; emphasis added.

In 1634 Thomas Sydserff became bishop of Galloway. He at once began to put pressure on the ministers under his jurisdiction for nonconformity to the innovations. First, he deprived eighty-year-old minister Robert Glendinning of his charge at Kirkcudbright by the Court of High Commission for refusing to allow one of Sydserff's "disciples" to use his pulpit. Only the intervention of his own son, one of the bailies of Kirkcudbright, prevented Glendinning from being imprisoned in Wigtown jail. Next, it was the turn of William Dalgleish, minister at Kirkmabreck, to be deposed for nonconformity. In 1636 Samuel Rutherford was deposed.[15]

Sydserff, a devoted follower of Archbishop Laud, was busily engaged at that time preparing an early draft of the new service book. It was dubbed "Laud's Liturgy," partly because Laud was believed to have altered it in many places.[16]

By the late 1630s, as opposition to episcopal innovations increased, the Southwest was much in evidence. Nor did Sydserff escape lightly for his actions. In October 1637, Edinburgh was the scene of large deputations of men from all the Southern counties: gentlemen, ministers, and burghers. Their purpose was to persuade the Edinburgh magistrates to join them in a petition to have the service book removed. While they were doing this, Bishop Sydserff was spotted. First, the mob subjected him to verbal abuse,[17] then they sought to manhandle him to reveal the crucifix he was said to wear beneath his vest. Only the intervention of some Southern nobles, themselves opposed to the service book, persuaded them to curb their actions. Sydserff escaped to Dalkeith.[18]

---

15. Morton, *Galloway and the Covenanters*, 63.

16. Morton, *Galloway and the Covenanters*, 64. The other bishops involved in the draft were Wedderburn of Dunblane and Maxwell of Ross.

17. Morton, *Galloway and the Covenanters*, 64. They insulted him with cries of "Papist loon! Jesuit loon! Betrayer of religion!"

18. Morton, *Galloway and the Covenanters*, 65–66.

Though Sydserff escaped the mob's clutches, a libel was brought against him at the general assembly in November-December 1638. As a result he was deposed from his office and excommunicated.[19]

The historic assembly of November-December 1638 received solid support in the form of attendance from the ministers, burgesses, and nobles of Galloway and the district around. This included the Earls of Galloway, Wigtown, Cassilis, Eglinton, and Dumfries, who sat in the assembly.[20]

At the parliament on August 31, 1639, which Charles I had agreed to, the Southwest was again well represented by the Earls of Wigtown, Galloway, Cassilis, Queensberry, and Annandale. Also present were Lords Kirkcudbright and Johnstone and the lairds of Largs and Kilhilt as representatives of Kirkcudbrightshire. Four commissioners also attended. The strict Presbyterians were in a large majority.[21]

As it was taken around the country, the National Covenant was welcomed enthusiastically in Galloway and widely signed. Every parish in that area had its own copy, though few are extant today. Those that exist include the Borgue Covenant, preserved in National

---

19. Morton, *Galloway and the Covenanters*, 69. His offenses included Arminian teaching; keeping a crucifix about his person; introducing anniversary feasts in his diocese; compelling ministers to accept kneeling at the Lord's Supper; deposing ministers for nonconformity; fining and confining certain gentlemen; embracing excommunicated papists and favoring them above Puritans; condemning the exercise of family prayer; being guilty of openly profaning the Sabbath; and engaging in secular business, such as buying horses.

20. Morton, *Galloway and the Covenanters*, 70–71. The following were also present: Samuel Rutherford, minister of Anwoth; William Dalgleish, minister of Kirkmabreck; John McClelland, minister of Kirkcudbright; Alexander Gordon of Earlston, Elder; William Glendinning, provost of Kirkcudbright; Robert Gordon of Knockbrex, burgess of New Galloway; Andrew Anderson, minister of Kirkinner; Andrew Laveler, minister of Whithorn; Andrew Agnew of Lochnaw, Elder; Alexander McGhie, burgess of Wigtown; John Livingstone, minister of Stranraer; James Blair, minister of Port Montgomery (Portpatrick); Alexander Turnbull, minister of Kirkmaiden; Sir Robert Adair, Elder; James Glover, clerk of Stranraer.

21. Morton, *Galloway and the Covenanters*, 71–72. The commissioners were William Glendinning, commissioner of the burgh of Kirkcudbright; Robert Gordon, commissioner of New Galloway; Patrick Hannay, commissioner of Wigtown; and John Irving, commissioner of Dumfries.

Archives and dated April 22, 1638. It contains a whole host of signatures, 152 in all, to which is added "with our hand at the pen by the Notar following at our commands because we cannot wrycht [write] ourselves." There follow thirty-seven more names, including Gavin Maxwell, minister at Borgue. Twenty-six names are appended to the ratification of the Glasgow Assembly of December 1638, endorsing that assembly's decisions.[22] In the old castle of Cardoness, at the mouth of the River Fleet, in the parish of Anwoth, three Cardoness Covenants, for years locked away in the Cardoness charter chest, have come to light. Again, a whole host of signatures is appended to them. One is known as the Miningaff Covenant, William Maxwell being the minister at Miningaff at that time.[23]

When the Covenanters divided into Resolutioners and Protesters, many of the ministers in Galloway sided with the Protesters. They would no doubt be aware of Rutherford's position, for he kept in touch with that area. Those who sided with the Protesters included John Livingstone, minister of Stranraer (from 1638 to 1648); John McClelland, minister in Kirkcudbright; John Semple, minister of Carsphairn; Lord Kirkcudbright; Adam Kae of Borgue; Thomas Wyllie of Kirkcudbright; Quentin McAdam; Alexander Gordon of Knockgray; and Captain Andrew Arnot.[24]

The Northeast of Scotland

Protestant doctrines found their way early to Aberdeen. The master of the grammar school, John Marshall, was summoned before the provost in 1521 for his contempt of the church. It appears he had imbibed some of Luther's teachings. He later recanted and submitted to the will of the burgh authorities.[25] In 1525, three weeks after the act of Parliament against heresy in Scotland, the king sent a letter to

22. Morton, *Galloway and the Covenanters*, 460–64.

23. Morton, *Galloway and the Covenanters*, 464–77. In 1662 Maxwell and the other Galloway ministers were turned out of their charges.

24. Morton, *Galloway and the Covenanters*, 81.

25. John Stuart, ed., *Extracts from the Council Register of the Burgh of Aberdeen, 1398–1570* (Aberdeen: Spalding Club 12, 1844), 1:98, 107.

the sheriff of Aberdeen and his deputies and to two of the principal burgesses of Aberdeen commanding that the act be published where needful in the diocese to stamp out the trafficking in "bukis of that heretik Luthyr" by "Sundry strangers and others within his diocese of Aberdene."[26] By the 1530s the new faith had infiltrated the ranks of the clergy. James V wrote from Aberdeen in 1534, complaining that "divers tracts and bukis translated out of Latin in our Scottish toung by heretics, favorers and of the sect of Luther" were being spread throughout the area.[27]

During the brief ascendancy of Regent Arran, a boost was given to the reforming party. In Aberdeen this took the form of the magistrates appointing two preachers of God's Word. Friars John Roger and Walter Thomson were appointed to preach and teach the true Word of God. A year later Roger was enticed to St. Andrews and was secretly murdered in the sea tower of the castle, becoming a protomartyr for the work of the gospel in Aberdeen.[28]

Contrary to what has been believed previously, the establishment of Protestantism in Aberdeen in 1559–1560 was not imposed from without but was indigenous. In particular, the merchants who were in constant touch with Reformers in Europe (see appendix 1), rather than the craftsmen of the town, were responsible for introducing the Reformed doctrines and worship.[29] By December 1559, it was reported that in Aberdeen "they have reformed their kirks, destroyed their altars, promised the destruction and abolishment

26. Stuart, *Extracts from the Council Register*, 1:110–11.

27. R. K. Hannay, *Acts of the Lords of Council in Public Affairs, 1501–1554* (Edinburgh: n.p., 1932), 423.

28. P. J. Anderson, ed., *Aberdeen Friars, Red, Black, White, Grey, Preliminary Calendar of Illustrative Documents* (Aberdeen: Aberdeen University Studies 40, 1909), 85; and John Knox, *History of the Reformation of Religion in Scotland*, ed. W. C. Dickinson (London: Nelson, 1949), 1:56.

29. Douglas Somerset, "The 'Alteration of Religion' in Aberdeen in 1559: An Ancient and Persistent Historical Error," *Scottish Reformation Society Historical Journal* 4 (2014): 52–53.

of the dens of iniquity."[30] It would appear that the elections for the Aberdeen town council in that year tipped the balance in favor of the Reformed faith, when four of the bailies returned were Protestant sympathizers. Douglas Somerset views this as "a warrant for reforming the burgh's public worship."[31]

One man who could have prevented or hindered this was Provost Thomas Menzies, whose family background was Catholic. He appears to have been more concerned to retain his position in local politics than to strongly espouse any religious beliefs. He has been described as "a man intellectually inclined to Protestantism, though tolerant of the practice of Romanism, and one whose main motivation was to retain power."[32] Another who could have provided strong opposition to Protestantism was the head of the House of Gordon, the fourth Earl of Huntly, the "Cock o' the North." Although initially of Catholic persuasion, his ambivalence in those crucial years was such that he at one point identified himself with the Lords of the Congregation, then shortly after, a year before his death, was offering to "set up the Mass in three shires" for Queen Mary.[33] By 1563, in Aberdeen and Banff, a Reformed staff at the very least of eleven ministers, eight exhorters, and sixty-six readers was in place (see appendix 2). Eighty-five out of ninety-one parishes in Aberdeenshire were holding Reformed services by the late 1560s.[34]

Once the kirk was established in the Northeast, a disadvantage was the lack of a divinity college for that area for training candidates for the ministry. There were two towns of Aberdeen at that time: Old Aberdeen, the "Aulton," inland a little and much smaller than the coastal town of New Aberdeen. Together they had a population approaching ten thousand, with between eight thousand to eighty-five hundred in New Aberdeen and around nine hundred in the

---

30. James Kirk, *Patterns of Reform: Continuity and Change in the Reformation Kirk* (Edinburgh: T&T Clark, 1989), 107.

31. Somerset, "'Alteration of Religion' in Aberdeen in 1559," 10.

32. Somerset, "'Alteration of Religion' in Aberdeen in 1559," 13.

33. Kirk, *Patterns of Reform*, 108.

34. Kirk, *Patterns of Reform*, 135, 153.

Aulton.[35] King's College and University in Old Aberdeen was founded in 1495. It remained solidly Catholic for a time after the Reformation. By 1569, however, King's College had been purged of its Catholic staff, "and although its production of ministers remained limited, this was rather more a consequence of having become a Protestant oasis in a still largely Catholic landscape than it was of lingering Catholicism in the college itself."[36] In 1593 Marischal College and University was founded by the Protestant George Keith, fourth Earl of Marischal. His main aim was to "provide a college which trained committed Protestant ministers."[37] Students and staff were expected to adhere to the Reformed faith. Eventually, divinity chairs were established at Marischal in 1617 and at King's in 1620.

Although the fourth Earl of Huntly was ambivalent, the fifth and sixth earls were decidedly Catholic in their stance and in their support. The House of Gordon had exerted its influence over the Northeast by diplomacy and marriage alliances.[38] Together—with its scions and their allies, like the Hays of Errol and in particular ninth Earl Francis Hay from 1595 to 1631—they were a dominant force in the rural Northeast. It was noted at the general assembly that one reason the Reformed church was not making the progress it would like in the Northeast was because the landed gentry of that area, many of whom were Catholics, tended to carry their tenants with them in their Catholic recusancy.[39]

---

35. Gordon DesBrisay, "'The civill warrs did overrun all': Aberdeen, 1630–1690," in *Aberdeen before 1800: A New History*, ed. E. Patricia Dennison, David Ditchburn, and Michael Lynch (East Linton, Scotland: Tuckwell Press, 2002), 239.

36. David Ditchburn, "Educating the Elite: Aberdeen and Its Universities," in *Aberdeen before 1800: A New History*, ed. E. Patricia Dennison, David Ditchburn, and Michael Lynch (East Linton, Scotland: Tuckwell Press, 2002), 330.

37. Ditchburn, "Educating the Elite," 330.

38. Bruce McLennan, "Presbyterianism Challenged: A Study of Catholicism and Episcopacy in the North-East of Scotland, 1560–1650" (PhD thesis, Aberdeen University, 1977), 63–64.

39. Thomas Thomson, ed., *Acts and Proceedings of the General Assemblies of the Kirk of Scotland* (Edinburgh: Bannatyne Club 81, 1839), 3:1025.

One way in which this recusancy was revealed was during rites of passage, such as baptism and marriage, when Catholics preferred to adhere to their old ceremonies, sometimes appearing before kirk authorities because of this.[40] Of the 835 Catholic recusants known to the kirk authorities between 1560 and 1650, three bore the title of marquis, four were earls, four were lords, four were barons, two were viscounts, and 130 were lairds. Sixty-three of the lairds were Gordons.[41]

The protective influence of the House of Gordon enabled secular and regular Catholic clergy to serve in the Northeast. In 1606, in a petition to the king, the Synod of Aberdeen complained of how the fifth Earl of Huntly and his barons and lairds had made the Northeast "the chief scene of that vain struggle to restore the ancient religion."[42] This continued unabated, so that in 1628 Father John Macbreck wrote to the general of the Society of Jesus that there was in Aberdeen at that time "a tolerably large mission attached to our Society" laboring in that area.[43] The work of this mission led to a letter from the government in Edinburgh to the Aberdeen magistrates, ordering them to stamp out the activities of the Jesuits: "Jesuit priests have come from overseas to Scotland, especially to Aberdeen… and are winning diverse converts…. Such [are] to be taken and imprisoned…also their conventicles to be stopped and the owners and masters of the houses where they are kept to be warded."[44]

The sixth Earl of Huntly, elevated to the marquisate in 1599, was a staunch supporter of the Jesuit priests. Right from the start of

40. Catherine McMillan, "'Scho refusit altogidder to heir his voce': Women and Catholic Recusancy in North East Scotland, 1560–1610," *Records of the Scottish Church History Society* 45 (2016): 40–47.

41. McLennan, appendix 2 of "Presbyterianism Challenged," 2:31–289.

42. Gilbert Blakhal, *A Brieffe Narration of the Services Done to Three Noble Ladies*, ed. John Stuart (Aberdeen: Spalding Club 11, 1844), xix.

43. W. Forbes-Leith, ed., *Historical Letters and Memoirs of Scottish Catholics, 1625–1793* (London: Longmans, Green: 1908), 2:33–34.

44. Edinburgh government to the Aberdeen magistrates (letter 270), December 2, 1628, in *Aberdeen Council Letters*, transcribed and ed. L. B. Taylor (London: Oxford University Press, 1942–1950), 1:295–96.

his accession, he offered his home at Strathbogie Castle as a base of operations for the priests.[45]

The First Episcopal Period

The time from 1610 through 1638 has been called the First Episcopal Period, 1610 being the date for the consecration of Scottish bishops in London.[46] It was during the episcopate of Bishop Patrick Forbes, Laird of Corse (1618–1635), that Aberdeen came to be recognized as the outstanding center of episcopacy in Scotland. In the early seventeenth century, two new schools of thought, or departures from the Reformed faith, found some fertile ground in the Northeast: Arminianism, which had its origins in Holland, and Erastianism, which had its beginnings in England.

During these years there were actually eleven men linked together who can be called the Aberdeen theologians of the First Episcopal Period, and not just the six known as the "Aberdeen Doctors."[47] Several of them—John Forbes, Robert Baron, and William Guild—espoused the same position as the Synod of Dort in their writings, though some of Baron's papers revealed leanings toward an Arminian position. Dr. William Guild held Anglo-Catholic views similar to Archbishop Laud. They were not, therefore, agreed on all points of doctrine nor were they all Arminian, as Rutherford regarded them.[48]

The Aberdeen Doctors, however, were very much in favor of episcopal innovations, as embodied in the Perth Articles. It appears that in the diocese of Aberdeen itself, the Perth Articles, especially the

45. W. Forbes-Leith, ed., *Narratives of Scottish Catholics under Mary Stuart and James VI* (Edinburgh, 1885), 206, 280.

46. Burleigh, *Church History of Scotland*, 207.

47. The six doctors were John Forbes, Robert Baron, William Leslie, all university professors; and James Sibbald, Alexander Scrogie, and Alexander Ross, ministers in Aberdeen. Then there was William Guild, William Forbes, Andrew Strachan, Andrew Logie, and Bishop Patrick Forbes himself. Ross and Scrogie contributed nothing in writing. Among them, the others produced thirty-seven works, most of them in the early seventeenth century. McLennan, "Presbyterianism Challenged," 1:223–358.

48. McLennan, "Presbyterianism Challenged," 1:272–75.

controversial one of kneeling at Communion, was being observed, as was private Communion.[49] Dr. John Forbes of Corse wrote in favor of kneeling and of the observance of certain festivals. Episcopacy, for him, was for the better ordering of the church.

When he was presented with the National Covenant to sign, John Forbes spoke for all his colleagues in *A Peaceable Warning to the Subjects in Scotland* in defense of their Erastian position. He maintained that the 1581 Negative Confession, which opened the argument of the National Covenant, was not legally binding, never having been ratified by Parliament. Indeed, the National Covenant had no parliamentary authority, no approval of the general assembly, and no royal assent.[50]

The Doctors defended their position as "Discovenanters" with the presentation of fourteen general demands,[51] which King Charles and his commissioner, the Marquis of Hamilton, were very pleased to receive. It sparked what might be considered the beginning of a pamphlet war between the Discovenanters and leading Covenanters Henderson and Dickson. The Doctors' argument was largely a legal one. What warrant did the Covenanters have for requiring subscription to the Covenant? Another major objection the Doctors had to signing was that in doing so they would be abjuring the Perth Articles, which they believed to be lawful and authorized by the sovereign. This debate was carried on in a most irenic spirit, the replies of the ministers being remarkably moderate and controlled.[52]

---

49. John Spalding, *Memorials of the Troubles in Scotland and England: A.D. 1624–A.D. 1645* (Aberdeen, 1851), 2:185. This is no doubt why Spalding makes a point of mentioning that when Andrew Cant administered Communion in Aberdeen, the recipients were *not* kneeling. *MS Records of the Kirk-Session of Aberdeen*, May 20, 1621; January 1631; December 11, 1631. CH2/448/1, 2, 3, 4.

50. McLennan, "Presbyterianism Challenged," 1:318–21.

51. These demands are given in detail in David Stewart, "The 'Aberdeen Doctors' and the Covenanters," *Records of the Scottish Church History Society* 22 (1984): 36–37.

52. McLennan, "Presbyterianism Challenged," 1:321–28; and Spalding, *Memorials of the Troubles*, 1:60.

Lynch and DesBrisay have pointed out how university staff tended to influence the way their graduates sided in the church conflict of the times: "Between 60 and 75 per cent of the ministers who graduated from the Presbyterian hothouses of Edinburgh, Glasgow and St. Andrews between 1616 and 1638 were to be found in the ranks of the Covenanters. Over half of the graduates from King's and Marischal, by contrast, opposed the Covenant."[53]

It was largely because of the teaching of the Aberdeen theologians and their works printed in Aberdeen by Raban that the town of New Aberdeen, even though there were definitely those who always sympathized with the Covenant, had decided to reject it before it was offered for signing.[54] John Row, minister in Aberdeen, commented, "The Doctors at Aberdeen were glad that their preaching and writing against the Covenant had so far prevailed with their people, as that they had in their Council refused to subscribe the Covenant, whereby they proceeded and laboured to withdraw all the subjects from it."[55]

On March 16, 1638, two commissioners from the Convention of Royal Burghs and three lairds presented a copy of the National Covenant to be signed by the New Aberdeen town council. The council refused because it fell "within the compass of contempt of his majesties royal authoritie."[56]

Two deputations of covenanting leaders to the north, however, in June and later in July, revealed that there was significant support for the Covenant, beyond what has been understood in the past. For example, most of the ministers of Caithness, Sutherland, Ross, Cromarty, and Nairn subscribed the Covenant.[57] As to the Synod

53. Michael Lynch, Gordon DesBrisay, with Murray G. H. Pittock, "The Faith of the People," in *Aberdeen before 1800: A New History*, ed. E. Patricia Dennison, David Ditchburn, and Michael Lynch (East Linton, Scotland: Tuckwell Press, 2002), 302.

54. *Aberdeen Council Letters*, 2:xi.

55. John Row, "A Supplement of the Historie of the Kirk of Scotland (1650)," appended to John Row, *The History of the Kirk of Scotland, from the Year 1558 to August 1637* (Edinburgh: Wodrow Society, 1842), 490.

56. DesBrisay, "The civill wars did overrun all," 243.

57. Jeffrey Stephen, "The Not So Conservative North: Covenanting Strength in 1638–39," *Scottish Reformation Society Historical Journal* 5 (2015): 68.

of Aberdeen itself, after a week of deputation work by Andrew Cant, minister of Pitsligo in Aberdeenshire, and his colleagues, subscriptions were secured from forty-four ministers from in and around Aberdeen, which was just less than half of the Synod.[58] Those who signed in 1638 did so out of principle; those who signed in 1639 did so more for pragmatic reasons, to keep their charges.[59]

With regard to the nobility of the Northeast, although the House of Gordon with its allies was strong, the covenanting movement had the support of the families of Forbes, Fraser, Keith, Burnet, Creighton, Innes, Grant, Tolquhon and Farquharson, and others.[60]

Stephen concludes on the strength of parties in the Northeast: "The Doctors in Aberdeen may well have been staunchly anti-covenant but they were not representative of the ministry in the north-east as a whole, and among that group there was considerable support for the Covenant."[61]

But at that time, the state of religion in that part of Scotland, and in the North in general, was given a far-from-flattering portrayal by Dr. John Forbes of Corse. He wrote of ministers being poor, of the order of deacons having lapsed, and many parishes being without readers and teachers. In some parts of the Highlands, the name of Christ was scarcely mentioned. Some ministers were "the most incapable and depraved of men." The universities and schools were not well attended. "Scotland," wrote Forbes, "was fast becoming a heathen field ripe for foreign missionaries, being absolutely bereft of those institutions of charity and culture which characterise a land once won for Christ!"[62]

This was the atmosphere in which Samuel Rutherford spent his time in exile, although he had departed south sometime in the spring of 1638. The confrontation between him and the Doctors

---

58. Stephen, "Not So Conservative North," 73.

59. Stephen, "Not So Conservative North," 74–75.

60. James Gordon, *History of Scots Affairs from 1637 to 1641* (Aberdeen: Spalding Club 1–3, 1841), 1:61; 2:211.

61. Stephen, "Not So Conservative North," 74.

62. Hewison, *The Covenanters*, 1:213.

will be covered in chapter 4. It is not surprising, however, to read of him giving expression, in the following terms, to his place of exile and why he was sent there specifically: "The lord hath brought me to Aberdeen, where I see God in few. This town hath been advised upon of purpose for me; it consisteth either of Papists, or men of Gallio's[63] naughty faith. It is counted wisdom, in the most, not to countenance a confined minister."[64]

This was a good example of Rutherford exaggerating. It has been pointed out recently that "Catholics were a tiny (if entrenched) proportion of the urban population; Arminians were a minority even among the clergy; and nowhere in Scotland did magistrates, ministers, elders and deacons urge the distinctively Calvinist crusade for 'godly discipline' with more rigour than in Aberdeen."[65] Rutherford also observed at that time that "our clergy is upon a reconciliation with the Lutherans; and the Doctors are writing books, and drawing up a common confession, at the Council's command. Our Service Book is proclaimed with sound of trumpet."[66] To Lady Kenmure he wrote, "I have heard a rumour of the prelate's purpose to banish me. But let it come, if God so will: the other side of the sea is my Father's ground, as well as this side."[67]

---

63. A reference to Acts 18:12–16, to Gallio, deputy of Achaia, who would not even listen to the religious dispute between Paul and the Jews. He "cared for none of those things."

64. Rutherford to Lady Boyd (letter 77), 1637, 163. Yet he could write somewhat later in that year, "I have gotten lodging in the hearts of all I meet with. No face that hath not smiled upon me." Rutherford to Lady Kenmure (letter 205), September 5, 1637, 402–3.

65. DesBrisay, "The civill wars did overrun all," 242.

66. Rutherford to John Livingstone (letter 90), February 7, 1637, 191–92.

67. Rutherford to Lady Kenmure (letter 230), September 5, 1637, 456.

3

The Life of Samuel Rutherford

Samuel Rutherford's life story has been told many times throughout the centuries, from the first substantial biography by Thomas Murray in 1828[1] to that of Kingsley Rendell in recent times.[2] Therefore, only a brief outline of his life is attempted here.

Rutherford was born around 1600. The place of his birth was Nisbet[3] within the parish of Crailing in the southeast of Scotland, four miles from Jedburgh in the presbytery of that name. Of farming stock, he and his two younger brothers, George and James, were educated at Jedburgh grammar school. George initially became a schoolmaster in Kirkcudbright and a reader in the church there. James was a soldier in European armies. From grammar school, Samuel proceeded to Edinburgh University in 1617, graduating with a master of arts in 1621.

It is important to note three formative influences that shaped young Rutherford's thinking with respect to church doctrine and government in those impressionable years. First, he came under the influence of David Calderwood, minister of Crailing from 1604 until 1617, when he was forced to resign his charge. Calderwood was very much in the Melvillian Presbyterian mold, like him asserting the independence of the church from the Crown for, as noted in chapter 1, there were two kingdoms. During King James's visit to Scotland in 1617, Calderwood protested the king's attempt to gain

1. Murray, *Life of Samuel Rutherford.*
2. Rendell, *Samuel Rutherford.*
3. Rutherford to John Scot at Oxnam (letter 344), June 15, 1655, 680.

control over the church. His stance against both episcopacy and popery were no doubt etched on Rutherford's memory.

While Rutherford was at Edinburgh University, he made the acquaintance and valued the friendship of two staunch Presbyterian merchants, John Meine and William Rigg. Rutherford would have observed how they absented themselves from services in Edinburgh, where practices such as kneeling at Communion were being introduced. They preferred to attend conventicles. These men were a second significant influence, and Rutherford later corresponded with them.[4]

A third but brief influence on Rutherford was that of Robert Boyd, a strict Presbyterian who had taught abroad in Europe, then in Glasgow, and then was principal of Edinburgh University from 1622 to 1623. In both his teaching and sermons at Glasgow and Edinburgh, he instilled in his young hearers, who included—along with Rutherford—David Dickson, John Livingstone, and Robert Blair, with whom Rutherford was to have long-standing connections, a love for the doctrines of grace and of Presbyterian church government.[5]

One of the features of college courses in those days was the regular debate and discussion that took place between professors and students. At this early age, Rutherford was given ample opportunity to develop his skills of argument and debate, which would later enable him to excel at the sessions of the Westminster Assembly in the 1640s.[6] Such was the impression he made on the university staff that only two years after graduating, he was elected professor, or regent, of humanity there, one of a handful of staff at that time.

Opinion has remained divided on two aspects of Rutherford's life at this time. The first concerns the fact that he was required to

4. Rutherford to John Meine Sr. (letter 151), March 14, 1637, 282; and Rutherford to William Rigg (letter 114), March 7, 1637, 230; letter 256, September 10, 1637, 501–3; letter 273, September 30, 1637, 529.

5. John Macleod, *Scottish Theology in Relation to Church History* (Edinburgh: Banner of Truth, 2015), 61; and Coffey, *Politics, Religion and the British Revolutions*, 31–37.

6. Rendell, *Samuel Rutherford*, 36.

demit his university post late in 1625. Many writers have simply glossed over this matter. In spite of some scandal regarding an irregular marriage to Euphame Hamilton, Rutherford did receive from the town council, patrons of the university, "an honest gratification at his dismission."[7]

Opinions also differ as to the time of Rutherford's conversion. Was his conversion precipitated by these events, as Coffey suggests, or was it as early as 1620? In a letter written from Edinburgh in July 1636 to the Viscountess Kenmure, Rutherford began by saying, "Noble and Elect Lady, that honour that I have prayed for these sixteen years, with submission to my Lord's will, my kind Lord hath now bestowed upon me, even to suffer for my royal and princely King Jesus, and for His kingly crown, and the freedom of His kingdom that His Father hath given Him."[8] He was writing in terms of entering into the fellowship of Christ's sufferings, something that loomed large in later letters. This is hardly the language of an unconverted man. Recently, Matthew Vogan has argued that his conversion took place when he was a student of eighteen or nineteen years, witnessing the stand taken by Edinburgh merchants like John Meine against the innovations happening at that time: "Rutherford could not avoid these events; he was at the epicentre of the unfolding drama relating to the protests against the Articles of Perth; and when his friends were being threatened and sentenced with banishment he tells us that he was praying to receive the same honour."[9]

His Pastorate at Anwoth

Whatever the truth of the above points of dispute, in 1627 Rutherford entered his only pastorate at Anwoth, in the stewartry of

---

7. For arguments for and against Rutherford leaving his office as regent because of fornication with Euphame Hamilton, see Coffey, *Politics, Religion, and the British Revolutions*, 37–38; and *Letters and Journals* of *Robert Baillie*, 2:342. Reference will be made later to letters that refer to the sins of his youth.

8. Rutherford to Viscountess Kenmure (letter 61), July 28, 1636, 136.

9. Matthew Vogan, "Samuel Rutherford's Experience and Doctrine of Conversion," *Scottish Reformation Society Historical Journal* 5 (2015): 41, 46.

Kirkcudbright, which would last only nine continuous years and then some months after his return from Aberdeen. His appointment was with the help of Sir John Gordon, later Viscount Kenmure, and Lord Lochinvar, who had originally wanted to see John Livingstone take up the charge. The appointment was accomplished without episcopal ordination.[10]

Before Rutherford's ordination, Anwoth had been linked with Kirkmabreck and Kirkdale, William Dalgleish being the godly and conscientious minister of this triple charge. He had labored assiduously in spite of the obvious difficulty of shepherding people over such a large area. Nevertheless, "not only the great body of the people, but the proprietors and higher orders had embraced the gospel, and showed it in their lives."[11] Rutherford, therefore, was the first sole pastor of Anwoth. The difference made by a settled pastor was brought out later in 1639, when an attempt in writing was made to try to keep him at Anwoth. The petition stated that before he came "our souls were under that miserable extreme famine of the word, that we had only the poor help of one most inconvenient union with other two kirks."[12]

The church building in which Rutherford preached was built in 1626 or early 1627. It was described some time later as "of a barn-like appearance, is one of the smallest and most humble we have seen, the length being 64 feet, 7 inches, the width 18 feet, 3 inches, the side walls only 10 feet, and being calculated to hold not above 250 sitters, exclusive of small galleries which are of comparatively recent erection."[13]

Murray notes that Rutherford's parish was "mountainous and extensive, and but thinly inhabited, and in which there was no village."[14] Nevertheless, people from the neighboring parishes were

10. Murray, *Life of Samuel Rutherford*, 36.

11. Murray, *Life of Samuel Rutherford*, 39.

12. Petition of the Parish of Anwoth, as quoted in Murray, *Life of Samuel Rutherford*, 355.

13. Murray, appendix to *Life of Samuel Rutherford*, note G, 357.

14. Murray, *Life of Samuel Rutherford*, 43.

soon traveling to Anwoth to sit under his ministry, particularly if they felt they were not being fed sufficiently well in their own parishes.[15] In addition, Rutherford was often invited to officiate in neighboring parishes at Communion seasons or fast days. Soon he was being looked on not simply as the minister of Anwoth but also as "the spiritual leader, guide and comforter of the whole province."[16]

Rutherford had no doubt that his call to Anwoth was in the will of the Lord, for he wrote to Marion McNaught, one of his regular correspondents, in 1631, "The great Master Gardener, the Father of our Lord Jesus Christ, in a wonderful providence, with his own hand (I dare, if it were for edification, swear it), planted me here, where, by His grace, in this part of His vineyard, I grow.... And here I will abide till the great Master of the Vineyard think fit to transplant me."[17]

John Livingstone, who had been Gordon of Lochinvar's first choice as pastor of Anwoth except he was committed elsewhere, wrote thus of the new pastor whom he knew and corresponded with:

> He used ordinarily to rise by three o'clock in the morning; he spent all his time either in prayer, or reading, or writing, or in visiting families in private, or in publick employments of his ministrie or profession. While he was at Anwoth, he was the instrument of much good among a poor ignorant people, many of which he brought to the knowledge and practice of religion, and was a great strengthener of all the Christians in that country, who had been the fruits of the ministry of Mr. John Welsh, the time he had been minister at Kirkcudbright.[18]

Using his imagination, Andrew Bonar pictures how Rutherford would lay aside his studies in early afternoon to visit his flock:

---

15. There were faithful ministers in some of the neighboring parishes: William Dalgleish in Kirkmabreck, John McLellan of Githron, and Robert Glendinning of Kirkcudbright.

16. Murray, *Life of Samuel Rutherford*, 46.

17. Rutherford to Marion McNaught (letter 16), n.d., 62.

18. John Livingstone, "Memorable Characteristics, and Remarkable Passages of Divine Providence," in Tweedie, *Scottish Puritans*, 1:320.

> See him setting out to visit! He has just laid aside one of his learned folios, to go forth among his flock. See him passing along yonder field, and climbing that hill on his way to some cottage, his "quick eyes" occasionally glancing on the objects around, but his "face upward" for the most part, as if he were gazing into heaven. He has time to visit, for he rises at three in the morning, and at that early hour meets his God in prayer and meditation, and has space for study besides. He takes occasional days for catechising. He never fails to be found at the sick-beds of his people. Men said of him, "He is *always* praying, *always* preaching, *always* visiting the sick, *always* Catechising, *always* writing and studying." He was known to fall asleep at night talking of Christ, and even to speak of Him during His sleep.[19]

In spite of Rutherford's obvious developing academic and scholastic abilities, to be among his people was to him an essential, integral part of his pastoral work. It was not enough to preach to them, as Andrew Thomson rightly observed: "He never dreamed his work was done after preaching. He was very sensitive to his position as an under-shepherd, appointed to take the oversight of souls. He therefore endeavored to know each individual member of his flock by personal intercourse, and to place himself in sympathy with each, that if any were afflicted, he was afflicted; if any rejoiced, he rejoiced also. He could therefore minister to their needs more helpfully, every parishioner regarding him as a friend."[20]

It is interesting to note the different preaching emphases of Rutherford and two of his friends and contemporaries, as described by a visiting English merchant around 1650. Robert Blair of St. Andrews revealed to this visitor the majesty of God; David

---

19. Andrew A. Bonar, "Sketch of Samuel Rutherford," in *Letters of Samuel Rutherford*, ed. Andrew A. Bonar (London: Oliphants, 1891), 5. In the last few lines of this paragraph, Bonar quotes James Urquhart, minister of Kinloss. A. Sinclair Horne, *Torchbearers of the Truth: Sketches of the Scottish Covenanters* (Edinburgh: Scottish Reformation Society, 1968), 15.

20. Andrew Thomson, *Samuel Rutherford* (London: Hodder and Stoughton, 1884), 25.

Dickson of Irvine, the oldest of the three, "showed me all my heart"; but Rutherford, by this time also in St. Andrews, " showed me the loveliness of Christ." This emphasis of Rutherford is seen clearly in his letters, particularly those written while in exile in Aberdeen.[21]

Episcopacy, an Encroaching Backdrop

When Rutherford began his pastoral work in 1627, episcopacy was already well entrenched in Scotland. In a letter to Lady Kenmure in June 1630, he wrote of "conclusions against such as are termed Puritans, for the rooting of them out. Our prelates…assure us that, for such as will not conform, there is nothing but imprisonment and deprivation…. Corrupt and false doctrine is openly preached by the idol-shepherds of the land."[22] He referred to the "false doctrine… openly preached" in a letter to another of his regular correspondents, Marion McNaught, wife of the provost of Kirkcudbright:

> The Lord hath let and daily lets me see clearly, how deep furrows Arminianism and the followers of it draw upon the back of God's Israel…. It is time now for the Lord's secret ones, who favour the dust of Zion, to cry, "How long, Lord?" and to go up to their watch-tower, and to stay there, and not to come down until the vision speak; for it shall speak (Hab. ii, 3). In the meantime, the just shall live by faith. Let us wait on and not weary.[23]

Three years later, in another letter to Marion McNaught, Rutherford complained that he believed the members of the presbytery of Kirkcudbright were turning cold toward him.[24] The explanation for this may be that in the same year, Thomas Sydserff, formerly bishop of Brechin, had replaced Lamb as bishop of Galloway. A convinced Laudian, Sydserff set to work to remove ministers who opposed

---

21. McCrie, *Sketches of Scottish Church History*, 372.

22. Rutherford to Lady Kenmure (letter 11), June 26, 1630, 53. Once the Court of High Commission was set up in 1610, the prelates had the power of imprisoning and depriving Nonconformists.

23. Rutherford to Marion McNaught (letter 17), n. d., 64–65.

24. Rutherford to Marion McNaught (letter 48), December 1634, 117.

his Arminian views. First, he tried to have elderly minister Robert Glendinning of Kirkcudbright imprisoned, but McNaught's husband, the provost, managed to prevent this. Next, in 1635 William Dalgleish was removed from his charge at Kirkmabreck. In March 1636 Rutherford himself was summoned to appear before the High Commission Court at Wigtown on a charge of nonconformity. This court deprived him of his ministerial office. Following this, he had to appear before the High Commission Court in Edinburgh. He described what took place in a letter to Marion McNaught, in which he also referred to his book that brought matters to a head:

> I am yet under trial, and have appeared before Christ's forbidden lords,[25] for a testimony against them. The Chancellor and the rest tempted me with questions, nothing belonging to my summons, which I wholly declined, notwithstanding of his threats. My newly printed book against Arminians was one challenge;[26] not lording the prelates was another.[27] The most part of the bishops, when I came in, looked more astonished than I, and heard me with silence. Some spoke for me, but my Lord ruled it so as I am filled with joy in my sufferings, and I find Christ's cross sweet.... Our bishop of Galloway said, If the Commission should not give him his will of me (with an oath he said), he would write to the king. The Chancellor summoned me in judgment to appear that day eight days.[28]

Shortly after this Rutherford wrote to Lady Kenmure that he was sentenced with deprivation and ordered to be confined within Aberdeen by August 20 "to remain during the King's pleasure, as they

25. He is referring here to the prelates with an allusion, perhaps, to the words of 1 Peter 5:3: "Neither as being lords over God's heritage, but being examples to the flock."

26. *Exercitationes Apologeticae pro Divina Gratia* (A defense of divine grace), published in Amsterdam in 1636. In a letter to one of his friends in Ireland, Robert Cunningham at Holywood, Rutherford wrote at that time, "The cause that ripened my hatred was my book against the Arminians, whereof they accused me, on those three days I appeared before them." Letter 63, August 4, 1636, 141.

27. By which he means not calling them lords.

28. Rutherford to Marion McNaught (letter 60), April 5, 1636, 135–36.

have given it out."[29] His "only exercise" was that he feared he had done little good in his ministry at Anwoth: "Only woe, woe is me, for my bereft flock, for the lambs of Jesus, that I fear shall be fed with dry breasts."[30]

Rutherford's stance against episcopal encroachments had nothing to do with political motives. Rather, it arose from "a deep conviction that such a hierarchy and the theological opinions which its abettors then entertained, were contrary to the word of God, and subversive of true religion."[31] His stance, however, ensured his exile, for he took a stand against innovations in liturgy, in doctrine, and in church polity. In all three areas he clashed with the Scottish bishops.[32]

Not content to remove the pastor, Sydserff proceeded against Rutherford's brother George, a schoolmaster and reader in the church at Kirkcudbright. He was summoned before the High Commission in Edinburgh in November 1636 to answer charges of nonconformity and support for persecuted minister Robert Glendinning of Kirkcudbright. The outcome was that he had to resign both as schoolmaster and reader and remove from the area. Murray notes that he "seems to have taken refuge in Ayrshire," close to where Lord Loudon resided.[33] There was a close spiritual link between the two brothers, but it was especially dear at that time of distress.[34] The concern Samuel showed for his brother's treatment and his appreciation for assistance and kindness shown to him from the time of his trial

---

29. Rutherford to Lady Viscountess of Kenmure (letter 61), July 28, 1636, 136.

30. Rutherford to Lady Viscountess of Kenmure (letter 61), July 28, 1636, 137. About the same time he wrote in a similar vein to Lady Culross—was he as faithful in the later years of his ministry as in the first two years, "when sleep departed from my eyes, because my soul was taken up with a care for Christ's lambs." Letter 62, July 30, 1636, 139–40.

31. Murray, *Life of Samuel Rutherford*, 92.

32. Coffey, *Politics, Religion and the British Revolutions*, 43–44.

33. Murray, *Life of Samuel Rutherford*, 93n.

34. Rutherford to a gentlewoman (letter 105), March 7, 1637, 218: "He is more to me than a brother now, being engaged to suffer for so honorable a Master and cause."

onward is reflected in his letters.[35] In return he prayed for those who gave assistance.[36]

Rutherford was not able to return to his flock. He made his way to Irvine for a brief visit with his friend David Dickson. From there, accompanied by some faithful members of his flock, he arrived in Aberdeen within the time set for him. The following chapter will consider his time in Aberdeen. With regard to his exile, DesBrisay commented, "The idea was that Rutherford, far from his base in the radical south-west, would find scant support in the conservative north-east, while exposure to the Aberdeen Doctors might have a softening effect."[37]

Rutherford's last letter from Aberdeen was on June 11, 1638. He was found preaching in the college kirk of Edinburgh early in June 1638 and then at the High Kirk of Glasgow along with Andrew Cant "to receave the oaths of the people to the Covenant, oaths they made with many a sigh and teare."[38] Rutherford was sent by the church to several districts of the country to publicize the cause of Reformation and the Covenant, highlighting also the way church members had suffered from recent innovations with the liturgy, book of canons, ordination, and the High Commission.[39]

When the free general assembly met on November 21 in the High Kirk of Glasgow, Rutherford attended as a representative of the presbytery of Kirkcudbright. At this assembly, eight of the fourteen

---

35. Rutherford to William Fullerton (letter 67), September 21, 1636, 146; to Earlston the Elder (letter 73), December 30, 1636, 156; to John Kennedy (letter 75), January 1, 1637, 160; to Alexander Colville, (letter 98), February 19, 1637, 205; to Lady Boyd (letter 107), March 7, 1637, 220; to David Dickson (letter 110), March 7, 1637, 226; to John Fergushill (letter 112), March 7, 1637, 229; to Lord Loudon (letter 116), March 9, 1637, 236; to Robert Glendinning (letter 136), March 13, 1637, 264; to William Glendinning (letter 137), March 13, 1637, 265; to Lady Busbie (letter 158), 1637, 292; to John Fleming (letter 159), March 15, 1637, 295; to Lady Kenmure (letter 205), June 17, 1637, 404; and to William Glendinning (letter 267), September 21, 1637, 518.

36. Rutherford to Lady Boyd (letter 245), September 8, 1637, 485.

37. DesBrisay, "The civill wars did overrun all," 242.

38. *Letters and Journals of Robert Baillie*, 1:89.

39. Bonar, "Sketch of Samuel Rutherford," 5.

prelates were excommunicated, four were deposed, and the remaining two suspended from their ecclesiastical duties.[40]

Rutherford's Move to St. Andrews

With the stature and ability that Rutherford had already shown, it is not perhaps surprising that he would not be allowed to remain in rural and remote Anwoth. He was soon in demand. First, Edinburgh requested of the commission of assembly his services as one of the ministers of that city. Then St. Andrews wanted him to be professor of divinity in the New College. The position proposed for him was in many respects the opposite of his quiet, rural country parish: "It was in truth one of the most important offices that a clergyman could fill. It was calculated to bring him into direct communication with the distinguished supporters of the Presbyterian polity, and to afford him a most favourable opportunity of impressing his own sentiments and views on the character of the church."[41]

The commission ordained him to be translated to St. Andrews. He had not sought this, though he may have been gratified by the recognition of his academic standing. What transpired at this point illustrates the deep bond that existed between pastor and congregation, which the exile for "six quarters of one year, during which space no sound of the word of God was heard in our kirk,"[42] had not diminished. Rutherford was unwilling to abandon a people to whom he was devoted and who had suffered much on his behalf. He presented to the commission a petition with eight reasons for staying. One reason of great weight in his eyes was that just as the lawful calling of a pastor required the consent, vows, and approbation of the people and presbytery, so also loosing him from his flock could not be without the consent and vows of the said flock and presbytery.[43] This was something Rutherford was very strong on. At the end of a letter written to the parishioners of Kilmalcolm at that time, he had

40. Murray, *Life of Samuel Rutherford*, 141–42.

41. Murray, *Life of Samuel Rutherford*, 159–60.

42. Murray, appendix to *Life of Samuel Rutherford*, note F, 355.

43. Murray, *Life of Samuel Rutherford*, 150–53.

written, "I must entreat you, and your Christian acquaintance in the parish, to remember me to God in your prayers, and my flock and ministry, and my transportation and removal from this place, which I fear at this Assembly, and be earnest with God for our mother-kirk."[44] To Viscountess Kenmure he wrote, "My removal from my flock is so heavy to me, that it maketh my life a burden to me: I had never such a longing for death. The Lord help and hold up sad clay."[45]

Rutherford's presentation to the commission was not successful. Neither was "the humble petition of Galloway" any more successful, though signed by ninety-five eminent landowners and clergymen in Galloway and some belonging to Dumfriesshire. Nor, further, did the petition of the elders and parishioners of Anwoth, signed by sixteen nobles and others, seven of them Gordons, with an additional 172 names that James Gordon, notary, appended, meet with a favorable result. They reasoned that they would not be able to support another pastor and that there were many recusants and papists in the area. A third reason was the bodily weakness of their pastor. A larger charge might be too much for him. Then fourth, and most importantly, they pleaded "ane mutuall union of our heart is betwixt him and us."[46] The last phrase surely sums up the love and devotion that existed between Rutherford and his flock, a bond neither wanted to break.

Rutherford yielded to the united desire of the church but "bargained to be allowed to preach regularly every Sabbath in his new sphere; for he could not endure silence when he might speak a word for his Lord."[47] The assembly acceded to this, appointing him to be colleague to Robert Blair, who himself had recently been removed from Ayr to St. Andrews against the wishes of both himself and his congregation.[48]

---

44. Rutherford to the parishioners of Kilmalcolm (letter 286), August 5, 1639, 564–65.

45. Rutherford to Viscountess Kenmure (letter 287), October 1, 1639, 567.

46. Murray, appendix to *Life of Samuel Rutherford*, note F, 353–57.

47. Bonar, "Sketch of Samuel Rutherford," 15.

48. Murray, *Life of Samuel Rutherford*, 161, 161n†.

Apart from the years 1643–1647, when Rutherford was one of the Scottish commissioners at the Westminster Assembly in London, St. Andrews was his home for the rest of his life. Robert McWard, who was to be his amanuensis while in London, described his first-hand impression of the situation Rutherford walked into. He was

> sent to the profession of Theology in the University of St. Andrews by the General Assembly...which being the seat of the arch prelate, was the very nursery of all superstition in worship, and error in doctrine, and the sink of all profanity in conversation among the students: where God did so singularly second his servant's indefatigable pains, both in teaching in the schools, and preaching in the congregation, that it became forthwith a Lebanon, out of which were taken cedars for building the house of the Lord through the whole land.[49]

Rutherford's contemporary John Livingstone likewise commended his work among the students and the congregation, the way in which he vindicated presbyterial government, "and in all his disputs hath no reflections on persons, but marvellously handles the point of controversie."[50]

Rutherford at the Westminster Assembly, 1643–1647

Rutherford was highly honored by his appointment as one of the commissioners, along with fellow ministers Alexander Henderson, George Gillespie, and Robert Baillie and ruling elders John, Earl of Cassilis; John, Lord Maitland; and Sir Archibald Johnston of Wariston. Yet the comments in his letters from the time reveal him to be far from at home in his London surroundings. He wrote to fellow minister Thomas Wylie of Borgue prior to his departure, "I am now called for to England; the government of the Lord's house in England and Ireland is to be handled."[51] How different were things from

49. Samuel Rutherford, *Joshua Redivivus*, ed. Robert McWard, 9th ed. (Glasgow: John Bryce, 1765), xv.

50. Livingstone, "Memorable Characteristics," in Tweedie, *Scottish Puritans*, 1:321.

51. Rutherford to Thomas Wylie (letter 306), October 20, 1643, 615.

Presbyterian Scotland! To Viscountess Kenmure he unburdened himself the following year:

> There is nothing here but divisions in the Church and Assembly; for beside Brownists and Independents, (who, of all that differ from us, come nearest to walkers with God) there are many other sects here, of Anabaptists, Libertines who are for all opinions in religion, fleshly and abominable Antinomians, and Seekers, who are for no church ordinances, but expect apostles to come and reform churches; and a world of others, all against the government of presbyteries.... I trust to be delivered from this prison shortly.[52]

He was not to be delivered shortly. The following month, in writing to Lady Boyd in the same vein and again recognizing the good spiritual character of those of a different persuasion from himself, he once more lamented the groups he was surrounded by: "Multitudes of Anabaptists, Antinomians, Familists, Separatists, are here. The best of the people are of the Independent way. As for myself, I know no more if there be a sound Christian, than if I were in Spain."[53]

Although unable to vote, Rutherford and his colleagues played an important part in the debates. Baillie, in fact, regarded Rutherford as "very necessary" for the work there.[54] The numbers of those who were not Presbyterians at Westminster prompted Rutherford to pen in 1644 *The Due Right of Presbyteries*. He did not believe in the gathered church principle of the Independents or Baptists. Sherman Isbell has in recent times, in analyzing Rutherford's book, ably defined the Presbyterian understanding of the church, to which Rutherford subscribed:

> The church visible is like a draw net, a workhouse of external calling. Rather than having in attendance only those who are already converted, the church visible is a place where hearers of the Word are brought under the care of pastors, and afterwards

52. Rutherford to Viscountess Kenmure (letter 308), March 4, 1644, 616–17.

53. Rutherford to Lady Boyd (letter 309), May 25, 1644, 619.

54. *Letters and Journals of Robert Baillie*, 2:159.

> are converted.... In Christ's parable of the tares and the wheat, Rutherford understands the field to be the visible church, in which the seed of the Word is sown. Rutherford envisages a church with many unconverted persons sitting under the preaching, and to such congregations the Puritans delivered searching sermons striking at the conscience. They preached against sin, invited men to come to Christ, and explained what were the distinguishing marks of a work of grace in an individual. The church visible is a company of the externally called, and being attached to it is a way of salvation.[55]

In the same year, 1644, Rutherford's *Lex, Rex, or The Law and the Prince* was published by authority in London. In it he stated clearly, "God hath given no absolute and unlimited power to a king above the law.... The power that the king hath...he hath it from the people who maketh him king." Then, with Stuart aggression in mind, he insisted that "absolute power to tyrannise over the people and to destroy them is not a power from God; therefore there is not any such royal power absolute."[56] With regard to the question whether the people can resist royal tyranny, he was quite clear: "How shall violence remove violence? Therefore an unjust king, as unjust, is not that genuine ordinance of God, appointed to remove injustice, but accidental to a king. So we may resist the injustice of the king, and not resist the king."[57]

Rutherford stayed the course at Westminster until 1647, being the last of the commissioners to leave London. The Westminster Assembly gave him this commendation to take back to Scotland:

> And now this reverend and learned professor of divinity, Mr Samuel Rutherford, signifying to us, that he is presently to returne to his particular station and employment among you,

55. Sherman Isbell, "Introduction to Samuel Rutherford's 'The Due Right of Presbyteries,'" in *Samuel Rutherford: An Introduction to His Theology*, ed. Matthew Vogan, Academic Series (Edinburgh: Scottish Reformation Society, 2012), 215–16.

56. Samuel Rutherford, *Lex, Rex, or The Law and the Prince* (Harrisonburg, Va.: Sprinkle Publications, 1982), 101, 102, 105.

57. Rutherford, *Lex, Rex*, 117.

> we cannot but restore him with ample testimony of his learning, godliness, faithfulness, and diligence; and we humbly pray the Father of spirits to increase the number of such burning and shining lights among you, and to returne all the labour of love which you have shewen to this afflicted church and kingdom, a thousand-fold into your bosomes.[58]

Troubled Final Years

In the last decade of his life, Rutherford continued his work in the New College, of which he became principal on his return. Four years later he was elected rector of the university. He continued his university duties but was also engaged in preaching, catechizing, and visiting. His amanuensis at Westminster and the first man to put out a collection of his letters in 1664, Robert McWard, referred in his preface to him as "exhorting from house to house, to teach as much in the schools, and spend as much time with the young men, as if he had been sequestrat from all the world besides: and to write as much as if he had been constantly shut up in his closet, so that one Mr. Rutherford seemed to be many able godly men in one, or one who was furnished with the grace and abilities of many."[59]

He remained firm to the end in his stance with the radical Protester group of Presbyterians, though there was never any thought of secession from the national church. When the church agreed to the policy of readmitting "Engagers," he found himself increasingly in isolation. He was surrounded by Resolutioner colleagues in the New College, in the church, and in the presbytery who did not share his Protester stance.

For some years his health had been in gradual decline. Indeed, it would seem that he was never blessed with a robust constitution. The period 1629–1630 had been a difficult time for Rutherford. He wrote to Marion McNaught in November 1629, "I am so comfortless,

---

58. Manuscript Minutes of the Committee of the General Assembly of November 26, 1647, as quoted in Murray, *Life of Samuel Rutherford*, 239.

59. Robert McWard, preface to *Joshua Redivivus: or Three Hundred and Fifty-Two Religious Letters, by S. Rutherford* (Rotterdam, 1664), xv–xvi.

and so full of heaviness, that I am not able to stand under the burthen any longer. The Almighty hath doubled His stripes upon me, for my wife is so tormented night and day, that I have wondered why the Lord tarrieth so long."[60] He enlarged on his wife's condition to McNaught shortly after that: sleepless, in great torment and pain night and day. He was now beseeching the Lord to take her home.[61]

The news of his wife's death, "after long disease and torment, for the space of a year and a month," was broken to Lady Kenmure, in which he also revealed to her how he had been "diseased of a fever tertian for the space of thirteen weeks." This recurring malarial condition had left him for a time able to preach only once on the Sabbath with difficulty. Nor could he visit or catechize his congregation.[62] Then, while Rutherford was still in his thirties, the eminent landholders and clergymen in Galloway and some of Dumfriesshire pleaded against his leaving Anwoth because "the weakness of Maister Samuel his bodie reqyres a lesser charge than he doth alreadie."[63]

The time spent in London was a stressful one. He lost two children by his first wife while in Anwoth; he lost two more while in London.[64] He lacked the fellowship of kindred minds, not feeling he could connect with many of those of different religious persuasions at the assembly sessions. The many duties in speaking and writing, of which he did not spare himself, must have taken their toll on his health. While in London, he and George Gillespie "took the waters" at Epsom, which gives meaning to fellow commissioner Robert Baillie's comment about the "variable state of his health."[65]

His decline is traceable in his letters. In one as early as 1650, which also reveals him to be in quite a depression of spirit, he

---

60. Rutherford to Marion McNaught (letter 6), November 17, 1629, 45.

61. Rutherford to Marion McNaught (letter 8), n.d., 49. He had sought medical help from Edinburgh from Dr. Jeally.

62. Rutherford to Lady Kenmure (letter 11), June 26, 1630, 53–54.

63. Murray, *Life of Samuel Rutherford*, 354.

64. Rutherford to Mistress Taylor (letter 310), 1645, 621.

65. *Letters and Journals of Robert Baillie*, 2:139; and Murray, *Life of Samuel Rutherford*, 235. Following the discovery of mineral waters in 1618, Epsom quickly became a popular destination for the restorative spa experience.

complained to William Guthrie, "I profess that I am almost broken and a little sleepy, and would fain put off this body."[66] The state of the nation and the divisions within the church played on his mind, so that he could write to Colonel Gilbert Ker, a prisoner in England, "For I have brought my health into great hazard, and tormented my spirit with excessive grief, for our present provocations, and the rendings of our kirk."[67] Three years later he wrote to Ker again: "For me, I am, as to my body, most weak and under daily summons;… as to my spirit, much out of court, because out of communion with the Lord, and far from what sometime hath been; deadness, security, unbelief, and distance from God in the use of means, prevail more than ever."[68]

He had always kept in touch with Galloway. Several letters went to Lady Kenmure. In one of them he wrote, "But my deadness under a threatening stroke, both of a falling church (a broken covenant, a despised remnant) and a craziness of body, that I cannot get a piece sickly clay carried about from one house or town to another, lieth most heavy on me."[69]

One of his last letters was to the presbytery of Kirkcudbright. After a passing reference to shortly putting off "this my tabernacle," he wrote with great humility, respect, and approval of the way that presbytery had tried to restore harmony between Resolutioners and Protesters: "I shall, in all humility, beseech your W[isdoms] to prosecute with the power which Christ hath given you the work of union." He did not live to see any healing or union.[70]

To Robert Campbell, fellow Protester and minister of a parish in the presbytery of Dunkeld, he wrote in his third-last letter: "For me, I am now near to eternity." He was still holding fast to his Protester

66. Rutherford to William Guthrie (letter 330), n.d., 653.

67. Rutherford to Colonel Gilbert Ker (letter 333), May 14, 1651, 661.

68. Rutherford to Colonel Gilbert Ker (letter 343), April 2, 1654, 678.

69. Rutherford to Lady Kenmure (letter 348), November 20, 1657, 683. Two years later he wrote to her again: "I was lately knocking at death's gate, yet could I not get in, but was sent back for a time." Letter 354, September 12, 1659, 688.

70. Rutherford to the presbytery of Kirkcudbright (letter 355), October 23, 1659, 689–90.

position,[71] as in his frail condition he put his last thoughts together and penned the "Testimony to the Covenanted Work of Reformation, in Britain and Ireland," written twelve days before his death. His position was the same as in *Lex, Rex*. While he was not anti-monarchical, he defended the right of the people of Scotland and England to have taken up arms in self-defense. He lamented the fact, however, that the king, having sworn the covenant and put his seal and subscription to it, had now gone back on his word. He disowned all the innovations in church services and was against even godly magistrates deposing men from the ministry.[72] As he reflected, however, on the way things were done, it would appear that toward the end he was beginning to think along the line of James Durham in his *Concerning Scandal*, when he wrote these words:

> It had been better, had there been more days of humiliation and fasting in Assemblies, Synods, Presbyteries, congregations, families; and far less adjourning commissions, new peremptory summonses, and new-drawn-up processes. And if the meekness and gentleness of our Master had got so much place in our hearts, that we might have waited on gainsayers, and parties contrary-minded; and we might have driven gently, as our Master Christ, who loves not to over-drive, but "carries the lambs in his bosom." [Isa. 40, 11][73]

Once the "Drunken Parliament"[74] had done its work of demolishing the acts of the Second Reformation (see chapter 1), it was the turn of men like Rutherford to receive attention. A number of copies of *Lex, Rex*, the book most offensive to the Committee of Estates, was publicly burned in Edinburgh and also in London.[75] Further

71. Rutherford to Mr. Robert Campbell (letter 363), n.d. but most likely 1661, 703–4.

72. Samuel Rutherford, "Testimony to the Covenanted Work of Reformation, in Britain and Ireland," appended to *Joshua Redivivus*, ed. McWard, 520–21.

73. Rutherford, "Testimony to the Covenanted Work of Reformation," 519.

74. So called because often "it was when they were stupefied by their carousels that the senators determined on their revolutionary enactments." Alexander Smellie, *Men of the Covenant* (Edinburgh: Banner of Truth, 1975), 59.

75. Murray, *Life of Samuel Rutherford*, 312–13.

action was taken against him. Murray summarizes it thus: "He was deprived of his situation as a member of the university, and of his charge in the church; his stipend was confiscated; himself ordered to be confined to his own house; and cited to appear before the ensuing parliament on a charge of treason."[76] When summoned to appear before them, Rutherford replied, "Tell them that I have a summons already from a superior Judge and judicatory, and I behove to answer my first summons; and, ere your day arrives, I will be where few kings and great folks come."[77] The summons came early on the morning of March 29, 1661.

76. Murray, *Life of Samuel Rutherford*, 314.
77. Smellie, *Men of the Covenant*, 63.

4

The Growth of a Soul

The time that Samuel Rutherford, "the banished minister,"[1] spent in Aberdeen was one of spiritual growth and of testing his doctrinal beliefs. Robert Gilmour wrote that "it is characteristic of the age of Puritanism that his banishment was to Rutherford a revelation of self."[2] The closer Rutherford got to Christ, the lower the opinion he had of himself. The words of John the Baptist could well be used to sum up his development in those months: "He must increase, but I must decrease" (John 3:30). He was tested not only by the contrasting circumstances in which he was now placed, bereft of his flock that meant so much to him, but also as to whether he would stay firm in his strong Presbyterian convictions in an environment that might well draw him from them.

Early Months in Aberdeen

Compared with Anwoth and Galloway, Aberdeen did indeed appear to Rutherford a strange, unchartered land.[3] In a letter to Hugh

---

1. Rutherford to Lady Viscountess Kenmure (letter 70), n.d., 150: "My garland, 'the banished minister' ashameth me not." This was how the people of Aberdeen described him.

2. Robert Gilmour, *Samuel Rutherford: A Study Biographical and Somewhat Critical, in the History of the Scottish Covenant* (Edinburgh: Oliphant, Anderson and Ferrier, 1904), 84.

3. Rutherford to James Fleming (letter 228), August 15, 1637, 453. James Fleming was minister of St. Bathans in the presbytery of Haddington, East Lothian. Rutherford wrote, "For He hath been pleased to open up new treasures of love and felt sweetness, and give visitations of love and access to Himself, in *this strange land*" (emphasis added).

Mackail, minister of the gospel at Irvine, he wrote of how Christ "would send me as a spy into this wilderness of suffering, to see the land, and try the ford."[4] He saw himself as sent not only into exile but also, like Joshua, to check out the land and report back to others. This gave Robert McWard the idea for what some might consider a strange title for his 1664 edition of the letters—*Joshua Redivivus*.

His first letter of around 220 from Aberdeen was written to Robert Gordon of Knockbreck, in the parish of Borgue, adjacent to Anwoth: "I am, by God's mercy, come now to Aberdeen, the place of my confinement, and settled in an honest man's house. I find the town's-men cold, general, and dry in their kindness; yet I find a lodging in the heart of many strangers.... Now, my dear brother, forget not the prisoner of Christ, for I see very few here who kindly fear God."[5]

In his early days there, Rutherford wrote of experiencing "great heaviness." One of the main reasons for this was "because it hath pleased the prelates to add this gentle cruelty to my former sufferings (for it is gentle to them) to inhibit the ministers of the town to give me the liberty of a pulpit."[6] This touched on that which was most important to the banished minister, something he often referred to: "The Lord knoweth, that I preferred preaching of Christ and still do, to anything next to Christ Himself."[7] "My witness is above that my ministry, next to Christ, is dearer to me of anything; but I lay it down at Christ's feet, for His glory and His honour as supreme Lawgiver, which is dearer to me."[8]

---

4. Rutherford to Hugh MacKail (letter 118), n.d., 240.

5. Rutherford to Robert Gordon (letter 66), September 20, 1636, 144–45.

6. Rutherford to John Fleming (letter 68), November 13, 1636, 147.

7. Rutherford to Lord Craighall (letter 86), January 24, 1637, 182. Similarly he wrote, "I had one joy out of heaven, next to Christ my Lord, and that was to preach Him to this faithless generation; and they have taken that from me." To Alexander Colville of Blair (letter 208), June 23, 1637, 408. Also he wrote, "My one joy, next to the flower of my joys, Christ, was to preach my sweetest, sweetest Master, and the glory of His kingdom." To James Hamilton (letter 214), July 7, 1637, 420.

8. Rutherford to John Row (letter 219), July 8, 1637, 429.

His desperate desire to preach to even a few comes out in a letter to John Stuart, provost of Ayr: "Oh, if I might speak to three or four herd boys of my worthy Master, I would be satisfied to be the meanest and most obscure of all the pastors in this land, and to live in any place, in any of Christ's basest outhouses!"[9]

Some of Rutherford's early letters, as he unburdened his feelings to others, reveal him questioning why Christ had brought him into this situation: "At my first coming hither I took the dorts [took offense] at Christ, and took up a stomach against Him; I said, He had cast me over the dyke of the vineyard, like a dry tree."[10]

He often referred to his silent, or "dumb Sabbaths,"[11] for he was grieved that he could not edify the Lord's people as before. But he also believed that his sufferings in silence could preach to the people of Aberdeen.[12]

Although he referred to Aberdeen as Christ's palace[13] in his early months, on several occasions he requested that his correspondents use their influence to enable him to return to Anwoth.[14] In a moment of weakness, perhaps, he let fall his desire to go to New England if he felt so called.[15]

---

9. Rutherford to John Stuart (letter 163), 1637, 305.

10. Rutherford to Lady Kenmure (letter 70), n.d., 150; also to Hugh MacKail (letter 71), November 22, 1636, 153; and to Alexander Gordon of Earlston, Elder (letter 73), December 30, 1636, 156.

11. Rutherford to Alexander Colville of Blair (letter 98), February 19, 1637, 205; to William Gordon of Earlston (letter 99), February 20, 1637, 207; to John Meine Senior (letter 151), March 14, 1637, 2282; to James Bruce (letter 146), March 14, 1637, 276; and to William Dalgleish (letter 184), June 16, 1637, 358.

12. Rutherford to Lady Viscountess Kenmure (letter 70), n.d., 150.

13. For example, Rutherford to Marion McNaught (letter 80), January 3, 1637, 168; and to Anwoth parishioners (letter 269), September 23, 1637, 523.

14. Rutherford to the Earl of Lothian (letter 83), 1637, 176–77; Rutherford to Lord Craighall (letter 86), January 24, 1637, 182; Rutherford to Lady Kenmure (letter 93), February 13, 1637, 197–8; letter 96, February 13, 1637, 202; and Rutherford to John Fergushill of Ochiltree (letter 188), 1637, 370.

15. Rutherford to John Stuart (letter 161), 1637, 301.

Gradual Acceptance

By the spring of 1637, Rutherford came to accept his circumstances. His change of heart and acceptance of his situation is seen in his letters at that time. To Lady Kaskeberry he wrote, "I am in this house of pilgrimage every way in good case: Christ is most kind and loving to my soul. It pleaseth Him to feast, with His unseen consolations, a stranger and an exiled prisoner; and I would not exchange my Lord Jesus with all the comfort out of heaven. His yoke is easy, and His burden is light."[16]

Rutherford had resigned himself to the providential hand of God: "I am now brought to some measure of submission and I resolve to wait till I see what my Lord Jesus will do with me."[17] What enabled him to accept his situation further was the firm belief he was suffering for the truth: "*The truth is, Christ's crown, His sceptre, and the freedom of His kingdom, is that which is now called in question.*"[18]

Greater Appreciation of, Love for, and Knowledge of Christ

There is much that is Pauline in the thinking of Samuel Rutherford. He appears to have had Paul's words to the Philippians very much in his mind at this time: "That I may know him, and the power of his resurrection, and the fellowship of his sufferings, being made conformable unto his death" (Phil. 3:10). The language of his letters was suffused with the expressions of marital love found in the Song of Solomon, what another has termed his "affectionate" theology.[19] Those who would be dismissive of such language would do well to

---

16. Rutherford to Lady Kaskeberry (letter 108), March 7, 1637, 222.

17. Rutherford to John Fullerton of Carleton (letter 157), March 14, 1637, 289.

18. Rutherford to Lady the Viscountess of Kenmure (letter 69), November 22, 1636, 148; emphasis added. He expresses this also in letters to Lady Kaskeberry (letter 108), March 7, 1637, 222; to John Fergushill (letter 112), March 7, 1637, 228; and to William Dalgleish (letter 117), n.d., 238.

19. This is a term used by Mark Dever in recent times that can be traced back to Richard Baxter. Guy M. Richard, "The Two Shall Become One Flesh: Samuel Rutherford's 'Affectionate' Theology of Union with Christ in the Song of Songs," in *Samuel Rutherford: An Introduction to His Theology*, ed. Matthew Vogan, Academic Series (Edinburgh: Scottish Reformation Society, 2012), 80–81.

heed the words of John Macleod: "When exception is taken to them [letters] on the ground that they use so freely the language of nuptial love, the critics, to be justified in their fault-finding, ought first to expunge from Scripture the Song of Songs, the forty-fifth Psalm, and much of the language in the Prophets, and in the New Testament which speak of the Lord as espoused to his church and of the church as his Bride."[20]

There is a sense in which Rutherford's spiritual development could not have taken place if he had not been removed from his Anwoth environment, bearing in mind his early rising to be with the Lord, his arduous study, then his constant visitation of the flock for various purposes. In much of this he would be expending himself for others. He confided to Hugh Mackail, minister of Irvine, "His dealings, and the way of His judgments, are past finding out. No preaching, no book, no learning, could give me that which it behoved me to come and get in this town."[21] In the same vein he wrote to John Fullerton of Carleton in the parish of Borgue: "It hath pleased His holy Majesty to take me from the pulpit, and teach me many things, in my exile and prison, that were mysteries to me before."[22]

Those who knew Rutherford well, like Viscountess Kenmure, who had benefited from his ministry at Anwoth and Kirkcudbright, might have been surprised at the way he indicated a desire to get closer to the Lord, regarding him perhaps as already learned and mature in the things of God. To Viscountess Kenmure, his regular confidante, he wrote, "It is little to see Christ in a book, as men do the world in a card. They talk of Christ by the book and the tongue, and no more; but to come nigh Christ, and hause [clasp or close with] Him, and embrace Him, is another thing."[23] A few months later, he wrote on the same theme: "Ye write, 'that I am filled with knowledge, and stand not in need of these warnings.'… Light, and the saving use of light, are far different. Oh, what need then have I to have the ashes

---

20. Macleod, *Scottish Theology in Relation to Church History*, 72.
21. Rutherford to Hugh Mackail (letter 118), 1637, 239.
22. Rutherford to John Fullerton (letter 157), March 14, 1637, 288.
23. Rutherford to Viscountess Kenmure (letter 69), November 22, 1636, 148–49.

blown away from my dying-out fire! I may be a bookman, and [yet] be an idiot and stark fool in Christ's way! Learning will not beguile Christ. The Bible beguiled the Pharisees, and so may I be misled!"[24] Rutherford was appreciating increasingly that the gift of salvation of itself was not enough, that he must continue to grow in grace and in the knowledge of the Lord Jesus Christ, something he would constantly impress on his correspondents.

Always frank and open in his letters, treating his correspondents as his equals—certainly never talking down to them, though he could be very stern when required—Rutherford unburdened himself in a remarkable way. He was prepared to admit that he was still very much a learner in spiritual matters; hence he would continue to grow. He began, therefore, by confessing that he had much to learn: "But I verily think now, that Christ hath led me up to a nick [point] in Christianity that I was never at before; I think all before was but childhood and bairns' play."[25] To Lord Balmerinoch he wrote that same month: "I am in Christ's tutoring here. He hath made me content with a borrowed fireside, and it casteth as much heat as mine own. I want nothing but real possession of Christ."[26]

His fellowship with Christ was growing. Rutherford wrote to Jean Gordon in that busy writing month of March 1637: "Oh, what sweet fellowship is betwixt Him and me! I am imprisoned, but He is not imprisoned. He hath shamed me with His kindness. He hath come to my prison, and run away with my heart and all my love."[27] Three months later he wrote to Lord Craighall: "I have found by experience, since the time of my imprisonment (my witness is above), that Christ is sealing this honourable cause with another and a nearer fellowship than ever I knew before."[28]

---

24. Rutherford to Viscountess Kenmure (letter 106), 1637, 219.

25. Rutherford to Alexander Gordon of Earlston (letter 97), February 16, 1637, 202. He wrote in a similar vein to Alexander Colville of Blair, adding he was enjoying communion with Christ as never before. Letter 98, February 19, 1637, 204–5. He wrote also to David Dickson (letter 110), March 7, 1637, 225.

26. Rutherford to Lord Balmerinoch (letter 139), March 13, 1637, 268.

27. Rutherford to Jean Gordon (letter 145), March 13, 1637, 275.

28. Rutherford to Lord Craighall (letter 174), June 8, 1637, 328–30.

His love for Christ was growing. Rutherford wished to be taken up with Christ Himself and not just His love to him—in other words, to be taken up with the Giver Himself, and not just what He had to give. "It is a pity that Christ Himself should not rather be my heart's choice, than Christ's manifested love."[29] On the first day of 1637, he wrote to his friend John Kennedy, bailie of Ayr, as follows: "I profess that I have never taken pains to find out Him whom my soul loveth; there is a gate [way] yet of finding out Christ that I have never lighted upon. Oh, if I could find it out!"[30] He was able soon, however, to sum up his first six months' exile in these words: "I never knew by my nine years' preaching, so much of Christ's love, as He hath taught me in Aberdeen, by six months' imprisonment."[31]

His view of Christ was growing. One of Rutherford's correspondents was John Nevay, minister of Newmills, in the parish of Loudoun, and chaplain to the Earl of Loudon. To him he wrote of how he had learned the joy of Christ's presence "now" and had not "frist" [postponed] it for a future meeting with Him: "For verily, brother, since I came to this prison, I have conceived a new and extraordinary opinion of Christ which I had not before." He urged Nevay to encourage young heirs of the kingdom to seek a greater and nearer communion "with my Lord Tutor, the prime heir of all, Christ."[32] The following month he wrote to Nevay, "I think better of Christ than ever I did; my thoughts of His love grow and swell on me."[33] In his sermon "The Apostle's Choice" (on Phil. 3:7–8), he said, "The more you enter upon thinking of Christ's fullness, the more will you love it. Paul, the longer he speaks of Christ, the higher he grows in estimation of Him."[34]

Rutherford sympathized with fellow ministers in Ireland, particularly those who had been deposed from the ministry for refusing

---

29. Rutherford to Alexander Gordon of Earlston (letter 160), 1637, 296.
30. Rutherford to John Kennedy (letter 75), January 1, 1637, 159.
31. Rutherford to John Gordon of Cardoness, Elder (letter 166), 1637, 311.
32. Rutherford to John Nevay (letter 179), June 15, 1637, 342.
33. Rutherford to John Nevay (letter 209), July 5, 1637, 409.
34. Rutherford, *Quaint Sermons*, 369.

to subscribe the canons that had been imposed on them.[35] One such was James Hamilton, deposed from the ministry at Ballywater. To him Rutherford wrote, "Certainly, since I became His prisoner, He hath won the yoke and heart of my soul. Christ is even become a new Christ to me, and His love greener than it was. I lay down myself under his love."[36] As he went deeper into the love of Christ, he was overjoyed by the love and joy he experienced, which he expressed to several of his correspondents.[37]

As the months passed, Rutherford's contentment in Christ so increased that he could write to his long-standing friend Marion McNaught, "A great, high spring-tide of the consolations of Christ have overflowed me.... His spikenard casteth a sweet smell. The Bridegroom's love hath run away with my heart. O love, love, love! Oh, sweet are my royal King's chains. I care not for fire nor torture."[38]

Growth of Humility and Self-Abasement

The closer Rutherford got to Christ, the greater was the awareness of the remaining corruption in his own heart and life and the utter vanity and emptiness of a world that no longer had any attraction for him. As his awareness of this grew, he would be able to relate the more readily to the various circumstances of his bereft parishioners and his other correspondents as one who had experienced, or was experiencing, something of the problems and challenges of life they faced.

He developed an acute awareness of his own sin. He had a growing realization of the guiltiness of his sins and of the sins of his youth. One of his correspondents who will be referred to later was his

35. Howie, *Scots Worthies*, 370.

36. Rutherford to James Hamilton (letter 214), July 7, 1637, 420.

37. Rutherford to George Dunbar (letter 265), September 17, 1637, 515: "I never believed till now, that there was so much to be found in Christ on this side of death and heaven. Oh, the ravishments of heavenly joy that may be had here." To Robert Lennox (letter 262), September 13, 1637, 512: "I can say more of Christ now by experience...than when I saw you. I am drowned over head and ears in His love."

38. Rutherford to Marion McNaught (letter 279), November 22, 1637, 540.

parishioner John Gordon of Cardoness, Elder, who had shown little concern for his eternal destiny. To him Rutherford confessed freely, "I never knew so well what sin was as since I came to Aberdeen, howbeit I was preaching it to you."[39] To John Stuart, provost of Ayr, he confided, "My guiltiness and the sins of my youth are come against me, and they would come into the plea in my sufferings, as deserving causes in God's justice; but I pray God, for Christ's sake, that he may never give them that room."[40] To Jean Brown, mother of the later well-known minister John Brown of Wamphray, in Annandale, he wrote of the power of sin that at times well-nigh overpowered him: "Sin, sin, this body of sin and corruption embittereth and poisoneth all our enjoyments. O that I were where I shall sin no more! O to be free of these chains and iron fetters, which we carry about with us! Lord, loose the sad prisoners!"[41]

His realization of the bondage sin could bring a person into seems to have produced in him humility and an estimate of his own worthlessness: "And what a slavery and miserable bondage is it, to be at the nod, and yeas and nays, of such a lord-master as a body of sin! Truly, when I think of it, it is a wonder that Christ maketh not fire and ashes of such a dry branch as I am."[42] He expressed his low view of himself most vividly in a letter to Lady Boyd: "I have seen my abominable vileness; if I were well known, there would none in this kingdom ask how I do.... I am a deeper hypocrite, and shallow professor, than every one believeth. God knoweth I feign not.... And, upon my part, despair might be almost excused if every one in this land saw my inner side."[43]

---

39. Rutherford to John Cardoness, Elder (letter 180), June 16, 1637, 346.

40. Rutherford to John Stuart (letter 162), 1637, 303.

41. Rutherford to Jean Brown (letter 84), 1637, 177.

42. Rutherford to William Glendinning, son of the minister of Kirkcudbright (letter 276), 1637, 535. Sydserff ordered Glendinning to be imprisoned for refusing to commit his father to prison.

43. Rutherford to Lady Boyd (letter 167), May 1, 1637, 313–14. He expressed his sense of his own sinfulness in a letter the same day to his friend David Dickson. In it he questioned "if Christ and I did ever shake hands together in earnest." Letter 118, May 1, 1637, 315.

The root of the problem, as far as Rutherford was concerned, was the master tyrant, "self." To John Fergushill of Ochiltree he insisted, "Oh, but we have much need to be ransomed and redeemed by Christ from that master-tyrant, that cruel and lawless lord, *ourself.*"[44] Writing to his ministerial friends in Ireland and sympathizing with their difficulties, he lamented, "O wretched idol, myself! When shall I see thee wholly decourted [discarded], and Christ wholly put in thy room? Oh, if Christ, Christ had the full place and room of myself, that all my aims, purposes, thoughts, and desires would coast and land upon Christ, and not upon myself!"[45]

Another feature in Rutherford's development, one that is a major theme in his pastoral advice, was his relationship to the world. His theme is basically reflected in the words of the apostle John, who wrote, "Love not the world, neither the things that are in the world. If any man love the world, the love of the Father is not in him" (1 John 2:15). Rutherford seemed to live as if waiting for his call to Immanuel's land. To Cardoness, the Elder, referred to previously, he wrote, "He hath made me to know now better than before, what it is to be crucified to the world. I would not give a drink of cold water for all the world's kindness. I owe no service to it: I am not the flesh's debtor."[46] He characterized the world as "a moth-eaten threadbare coat...and full of holes."[47] Similarly, he wrote to Lord Balmerinoch, "Now, my Lord, I must tell your Lordship that I would not give a drink of cold water for this clay idol, this plastered world."[48] Writing back to his parishioner John Gordon of Rusco, he said, "For I find this world, when I have looked upon it on both sides, within and without, and when I have seen even the laughing and lovely side of

44. Rutherford to John Fergushill (letter 188), 1637, 370.

45. Rutherford to the professors of Christ and His truth in Ireland (letter 284), February 4, 1638, 554.

46. Rutherford to Cardoness, the Elder (letter 166), 1637, 311.

47. Rutherford to William Gordon of Earlston, Younger (letter 99), February 20, 1637, 208.

48. Rutherford to Lord Balmerinoch (letter 139), March 13, 1637, 268.

it, to be but a fool's idol, a clay prison. Lord, let it not be the nest that my hope buildeth in."[49]

One feature of Rutherford's correspondence, which will be developed further in part 2, is that of the "crosses" to which believers are subjected. For himself, in particular, his crosses were to be separated from his flock, not knowing how they would be fed; to be banished to a very different environment where he was surrounded by papists and Arminians; and to be forbidden to preach. Rutherford, however, saw crosses as predetermined. To one of his parishioners, Margaret Reid, he wrote, "Ere ye were born, crosses, in number, measure, and weight, were written for you, and your Lord will lead you through them."[50]

The purpose of crosses in their mortifying and sanctifying effect he enlarged on to Lady Craighall: "I know that Christ bought with His own blood a right to sanctified and blessed crosses, in so far as they blow me over the water to my long-desired home. Christ's cross shall have my testimonial under my hand, as an honest and saving mean of Christ for mortification and faith's growth. I have a stronger assurance, since I came over the Forth, of the excellency of Jesus, than I had before."[51] He had always lived south of the River Forth up till this time.

Even more than this, he viewed his cross as "neither a cruel nor unkind mercy, but the love-token of a Father."[52] He was confident that he would not be tested beyond that which he could bear: "Not one ounce, not one grain-weight more is laid on me than He hath enabled me to bear; and I am not so much wearied to suffer as Zion's haters are to persecute."[53]

---

49. Rutherford to John Gordon of Rusco (letter 272), 1637, 527.

50. Rutherford to Margaret Reid (letter 248), n.d., 488.

51. Rutherford to Lady Craighall (letter 257), September 10, 1637, 503–4.

52. Rutherford to William Gordon of Roberton (letter 72), 1637, 155.

53. Rutherford to William Rigg (letter 114), March 9, 1637, 231. Rigg was one of the staunch opponents of episcopacy and at one time was a bailie in Edinburgh. He was also noted for devoting a large portion of his income to religious causes.

Rutherford and the Doctors

Rutherford's strict Presbyterian stance brought him into dispute with the Doctors.[54] He was required, first, to attend divine service in the college kirk beside Marischal College and University. He referred to this in a letter to his friend Robert Blair in February 1637: "I am here a prisoner confined in Aberdeen, threatened to be removed to Caithness, because I desire to edify in this town; and am openly preached against in the pulpits in my hearing, and tempted with disputations by the doctors, especially by D. B. Yet I am not ashamed of the Lord Jesus, His garland, and His crown."[55]

D. B., Dr. Robert Baron, a major exponent of Arminianism, was indeed his first opponent. Their debate centered first on the doctrines of grace. Baron sought to deny the predestination of man's sins, whereas Rutherford contended for an absolute predestination as bringing most glory to God. Second, Baron contended to prove that Christ died for all men indiscriminately, whereas Rutherford contended that Christ belonged to only believing sinners who had trusted in Christ. His Scripture proofs were John 1:12; Ephesians 3:17; and Galatians 2:20. A third point of dispute was the will, with Baron contending for free will and Rutherford for the total depravity of man, whose will was in bondage. Faith, Baron maintained, was a free

54. The early Reformers were not against reviving the medieval doctorate of divinity. The general assembly in 1569 invited the colleges of St. Andrews to submit regulations for that degree. Five years later the assembly was recommending that "Doctouris may be placit at Universities." The first was at St. Andrews in 1616, then in 1620 Aberdeen's Principal Rait of King's College received the degree. The "Aberdeen Doctors," three of them professors (John Forbes, Robert Baron, and William Leslie) and three of them ministers in Aberdeen (James Sibbald, Alexander Scrogie, and Alexander Ross) all took the doctorate of divinity at King's College by thesis. Thomson, *Acts and Proceedings of the General Assemblies*, 1:305; David Calderwood, *History of the Kirk of Scotland*, ed. Thomas Thomson (Edinburgh: Wodrow Society, 1842–49), 3:563n; G. D. Henderson, *Religious Life in Seventeenth Century Scotland* (Cambridge: Cambridge University Press, 1937), 43; G. D. Henderson, *The Burning Bush* (Edinburgh: Saint Andrew Press, 1957), 85.

55. Rutherford to Robert Blair (letter 89), February 7, 1637, 189.

act, whereas Rutherford maintained that faith was wrought in the repentant sinner by the saving grace of God.[56]

A second point of dispute concerned the service book that the professors at Aberdeen had been charged to draw up. Baron defended it on the basis that it had royal authorization. Rutherford replied that "arbitrary power is a fit garland only for Infinite Majesty." Rutherford wrote to his colleague William Dalgleish, "Dr. Barron hath often disputed with me, especially about Arminian controversies, and for the ceremonies. Three yokings laid him by; and I have not been troubled with him since."[57] A further dispute took place with Dr. Sibbald, whose Arminian views were well known. Rutherford maintained that man is justified not by an inherent righteousness but by the righteousness of Christ freely imputed to him.[58]

Rutherford summed up his encounters in a letter to his close friend and colleague in the ministry George Gillespie: "I am here troubled with the disputes of the great doctors (especially with Dr. B.) in Ceremonial and Arminian controversies, for all are corrupt here; *but, I thank God, with no detriment to the truth, or discredit to my profession.*"[59]

Time Profitably Spent in Aberdeen

Even though Rutherford was not allowed to occupy a pulpit, the time from autumn 1636 to late spring 1638 was nevertheless very busy. Letter writing, of course, was one preoccupation. He wrote to Hugh Mackail of Irvine in September 1637, "I cannot, for the multitude of letters and distraction of friends, prepare what I would for the times: I have not one hour of spare time, suppose the day were forty

---

56. John M. Brentnall, *Samuel Rutherford in Aberdeen* (Inverness: John G. Eccles, 1981), 133–35: John M. Brentnall, *Puritan and Covenanter Studies* (Swanick, Derbyshire, England: John M. Brentnall, n.d.), 10–11.

57. Rutherford to William Dalgleish (letter 117), n.d., 238.

58. Brentnall, *Samuel Rutherford in Aberdeen*, 136–38; and Brentnall, *Puritan and Covenanter Studies*, 12–14.

59. Rutherford to George Gillespie (letter 144), March 13, 1637, 275; emphasis added.

hours long."[60] Two days later he confided to fellow minister James Hamilton, "I am exceedingly distracted with letters, and company that visit me: what I can do, or time will permit, I shall not omit. Excuse my brevity, for I am straitened."[61] This is in contrast to his complaint at the start of his time in exile that he was not receiving much in the way of correspondence from Galloway.[62] This had obviously changed, as he received a continuous stream of letters that he no doubt felt obliged to answer. It may be that some letters never reached their intended destination in Aberdeen or his replies sent to Galloway and other places. The letters that he wrote, particularly the 220 or so written from Aberdeen, may be seen as a continuation of the personal visitation and one-on-one counseling that had been such an essential part of Rutherford's pastoral work in Anwoth.

Although not permitted to occupy a pulpit in Aberdeen, he nevertheless spoke of an impression made on the townsfolk. Aberdonians seeking spiritual help came to him in Burn Court in the Upperkirkgate.[63] Indeed, his very deportment, his "conversation," or manner of life in the town, must have made a distinct impression on the people, for he wrote to John Stuart, provost of Ayr, "He hath been pleased in my sufferings to make Atheists, Papists, and enemies about me say, 'It is like that God is with this prisoner.'"[64] His personal witnessing had borne some fruit. He wrote to Marion McNaught of "some blossomings of Christ's kingdom in this town," which aroused the anger of the ministers.[65] To his close friend David Dickson he

60. Rutherford to Hugh Mackail (letter 229), September 5, 1637, 455.

61. Rutherford to James Hamilton (letter 236), September 7, 1637, 471.

62. Rutherford to Marion McNaught (letter 80), January 3, 1637, 168: "I complain that Galloway is not kind to me in paper. I have received no letters these sixteen weeks but two." The following month he wrote to Alexander Gordon of Earlston: "I received your letter, which refreshed me. Except from your son, and my brother, I have seen few letters from my acquaintance in that country; which maketh me heavy." Letter 97, February 16, 1637, 202.

63. Brentnall, *Samuel Rutherford in Aberdeen*, 19; and Brentnall, *Puritan and Covenanter Studies*, 146.

64. Rutherford to John Stuart (letter 162), 1637, 203.

65. Rutherford to Marion McNaught (letter 243), September 7, 1637, 480.

noted "a little brairding [sprouting up] of God's seed in this town."[66] He also had the support of certain of the nobility in the area. For example, he wrote in June 1637, "My Lady Marischall is very kind to me, and her son also."[67] The son was William, soon to become the seventh Earl Marischall.

By May 1637, he was holding prayer meetings in his lodgings on a regular basis. He wrote to Sir John Moncrieff, a ruling elder in the parish of Carnbee and a zealous Covenanter, asking for a concert of prayer "with us (so many as in these bounds profess Christ), to wrestle with God, one day of the week, especially the Wednesday, for mercy to this fallen and decayed kirk, and to such as suffer for Christ's name."[68] Many people were moved to supplicate the town council to permit him to return home.[69]

Such was the impact that Rutherford had made during his exile and during a return visit to Aberdeen for the general assembly in 1640, when they met in the Greyfriars Kirk "with the avowed intention of bringing the remaining doctors and ministers to the obedience of the kirk,"[70] that it seems they wanted him back. In 1644 the provost and council of Aberdeen asked him to replace Dr. Baron[71] as professor of divinity at Marischal College, with preaching responsibilities also in the college kirk. By that time, however, Rutherford was firmly established in New College, St. Andrews, and that very year, in fact, was with the Scots commissioners at the Westminster Assembly in London.[72]

---

66. Rutherford to David Dickson (letter 259), September 11, 1637, 508.

67. Rutherford to Viscountess Kenmure (letter 206), June 17, 1637, 407.

68. Rutherford to Sir John Moncrieff (letter 171), May 14, 1637, 321.

69. Rutherford to Marion McNaught (letter 243), September 7, 1637, 480.

70. McLennan, *Presbyterianism Challenged*, 1:350.

71. At the approach of the army of the Covenant, people began to seek safety in flight. The first to leave were the three doctors Leslie, Sibbald, and Baron, who, in the company of about sixty youths and men who intended to serve their king down south, left Aberdeen on March 28, 1639. Some country ministers followed their example. Baron made it south only as far as Berwick, dying there in August 1639. Gordon, *History of Scots Affairs*, 2:225; and McLennan, *Presbyterianism Challenged*, 1:341–42.

72. Brentnall, *Samuel Rutherford in Aberdeen*, 22–23; and Brentnall, *Puritan and Covenanter Studies*, 151.

PART 2

The Pastoral Work of Samuel Rutherford

Part 2 considers key recurring emphases in Rutherford's correspondence, sermons, and writings and then brings out the strong pastoral concern Rutherford had for his own bereft flock. He conducted himself in this respect in very much the same spirit as if he were still in their midst. Never content when his time of preaching had ended, he reasoned with souls to make their calling and election sure, to follow after holiness, putting much emphasis on sanctification and mortification. Various individuals and groups received his spiritual counsel, including those farther afield in Scotland, England, and Ireland. His concern extended from the very young to those who were dying.

5

Key Emphases in Rutherford's Writings

Most of those familiar with Samuel Rutherford's writings have seen in them, and particularly in his letters, the way in which his appreciation of the loveliness of Christ shines forth as a main feature. No matter what the subject of a particular piece of correspondence was, Rutherford expressed his love for the Lord Jesus and his desire to continually praise Him, extol Him to others, and enter more deeply into the knowledge of Him. This was particularly so during his "exile" in Aberdeen. Maurice Roberts has well remarked, "Anwoth taught him to enjoy Christ, with the emphasis on the future world of glory. Aberdeen was the palace of gold where he learned to enjoy Christ with an emphasis not only on the future but on the present."[1] Many examples could be given of the way he extolled Christ and of his desire for closer fellowship with Him. A few must suffice:

> He is become a new Well-beloved to me now, in renewed consolations, by the presence of the Spirit of grace and glory. Christ's garments smell of the powder of the merchant, when He cometh out of His ivory chambers. Oh, His perfumed face, His fair face, His lovely and kindly kisses, have made me, a prisoner, see that there is more to be had of Christ in this life than I believed![2]

1. Maurice Roberts, "Samuel Rutherford: 'The Comings and Goings of the Heavenly Bridegroom,'" in *The Trials of Puritanism,* by Samuel T. Logan Jr. et al, Westminster Conference Papers, 1993 (Mirfield: Westminster Conference Secretary, [1994]), 128.

2. Rutherford to Viscountess Kenmure (letter 94), 1637, 199.

> Come in, come in to Christ, and see what ye want, and find in Him.... I think His sweetness, since I was a prisoner, hath swelled upon me to the greatness of two heavens. Oh for a soul as wide as the utmost circle of the highest heaven that containeth all, to contain his love! And yet I could hold little of it. O world's wonder! Oh, if my soul might but lie within the smell of His love, suppose I could get no more but the smell of it! Christ, Christ, nothing but Christ, can cool our love's burning languor. O thirsty love! Wilt thou set Christ, the well of life, to thy head, and drink thy fill? Drink, and spare not; drink love, and be drunken with Christ![3]

> O thou fair and fairest Sun of righteousness, arise and shine in thy strength, whether earth or hell will or not. O victorious, O royal, O stout, princely Soul-conqueror, ride prosperously upon truth; stretch out Thy sceptre as far as the sun shineth, and the moon waxeth and waneth. Put on Thy glittering crown, O Thou maker of kings, and make but one stride, of one step of the whole earth, and travel in the greatness of Thy strength. (Isa. Lxii, 1, 2)[4]

Rutherford's experience of the presence of Christ was not constant. He understood this in terms of the Song of Solomon because he saw the relationship between the believer and Christ depicted there and loved to preach from that book, which portrayed Christ's comings and goings, or desertions. He explained it in this way in his *Christ Dying and Drawing Sinners to Himself*: "Therefore often the time of some extreme desertion and soul trouble is, when Christ hath been in the soul with a full high spring-tide of divine manifestations of Himself." He used by illustration the apostle Paul after he had been caught up to the third heaven: "God thinketh then good to exercise him with a messenger of Satan, which by the weakness and spiritual infirmity he was under, wanted not a desertion, less

3. Rutherford to John Gordon of Cardoness, Elder (letter 82), 1637, 173.

4. Rutherford to Henry Stuart, his wife, and two daughters, all prisoners of Christ at Dublin (letter 291), 1640, 584.

or more, whatever the messenger was."[5] From his own experience, he wrote to James Fleming, minister of Abbey St. Bathans in East Lothian, "I never find myself nearer Christ, that royal and princely One, than after a great weight and sense of deadness and graceless-ness. I think that the sense of our wants, when withal we have a sort of restlessness and a sort of spiritual impatience…because we want Him whom our soul loveth, is that which maketh an open door to Christ."[6] His advice, therefore, to another of his correspondents, Lady Cardoness, was when Christ hides Himself, "wait on, and make a din till He return."[7]

The Sovereignty of God

God's sovereignty is an emphasis that pervaded Rutherford's thinking and writing. He was a convinced supralapsarian, holding that God creates some people for destruction without regard to their sin, having already decreed to pass them over. His "understanding of salvation, likewise, exalts the freedom of God's will over human freedom."[8] He believed his supralapsarian stance brought most glory to God.

"What is sovereignty?" asked Rutherford in his *Influences of the Life of Grace*. His answer: "It's his super excellent Highness by which his holy Will essentially wise and just, is a Law and Rule to Himself to do what he pleaseth, holily, wisely, most freely."[9] He distinguished sovereignty from omnipotency: "Omnipotency looks simply to effects physically, what the lord can doe; he can of stones make sons to Abraham; he can create millions of Worlds; His sovereignty is not only his holy Nature what he can doe and so supposeth his Omnipo-tency, but also what he doth freely, or doth not freely, and doth by

5. Samuel Rutherford, *Christ Dying and Drawing Sinners to Himself* (Zeeland, Mich.: Reformed Church Publications, 2009), 50. He then went on to expound Song of Solomon 5.

6. Rutherford to James Fleming (letter 228), August 15, 1637, 453.

7. Rutherford to Lady Cardoness (letter 100), February 20, 1637, 209–10.

8. Richard, *Supremacy of God*, 219.

9. Samuel Rutherford, *Influences of the Life of Grace* (London: Andrew Crook, 1658), 34–35.

no natural necessity, and so it includes his holy supreme Liberty, and also what the Lord may doe."[10] Rutherford further declared that sovereignty and the glorious liberty of God was to be seen in His decrees of election and reprobation as illustrated in His love for Jacob and hatred of Esau before the children had done good or evil.[11]

For those who had difficulties with God's sovereign purposes, Rutherford had this advice in the preface to his *Influences*: "Some are troubled how Sovereignty of quickening influences in the gratious Lord, who quickens hic and nunc, in every duty, and withdraws his sovereign concurrence as he best pleaseth, can consist with our debt of duty. It's safest to look to duty and the commanding will to rise up and be doing, and not to dazzle the wit with disputing the sovereignty of God, nor to enquire into his latent decreeing will."[12]

His emphasis on God's sovereignty comes out repeatedly in his correspondence. For example, he acknowledged God to be in control of events, even when He appeared to have withdrawn Himself and the kirk was going through a dark period. Such a time was 1653, when Rutherford wrote as follows to Colonel Gilbert Ker in England: "The causes of His withdrawings are unknown to us. One thing cannot be denied, but that the ways of high sovereignty and dominion of grace are far out of the sight of angels and men."[13] With regard to salvation itself, even in the course of pleading with souls to seek the Lord in earnest, he could write, as he did to John Gordon of Cardoness, Elder, that "salvation is not casten down at every man's door,"[14] a phrase found often in his writing. Or, when comforting some who had recently been bereaved, as will be referred to later, he could counsel them to accept that God's sovereignty was at work: "I believe faith will teach you to kiss a striking Lord; and so acknowledge the sovereignty of God (in the death of a child) to be above the

10. Rutherford, *Influences of the Life of Grace*, 33.

11. Rutherford, *Influences of the Life of Grace*, 45.

12. Rutherford, "Address to the Godly Reader," in *Influences of the Life of Grace*, point 3, n.p.

13. Rutherford to Colonel Gilbert Ker (letter 342), July 1653, 675.

14. Rutherford to John Gordon of Cardoness, Elder (letter 82), 1637, 171.

power of us mortal men, who may pluck up a flower in the bud and not be blamed for it."[15]

The Providence of God

In his catechism, Samuel Rutherford began chapter 9 with the question, "What is the second work whereby God brings His decrees to pass?" Answer—"By the work of his providence and government of the world." This definition is then developed into three parts, giving several Scripture proofs for each: first, He bears up all things in his arms else they would turn to nothing; second, He sets all things that work and move to work; third, by His eternal wisdom and power He directs all things, even sin, to His own glory.[16]

A phrase found several times in Rutherford's correspondence summarizes his approach to providence: "Duties are ours, events are the Lord's."[17] It was something he confessed to learning by experience himself, as he wrote from Aberdeen to Alexander Gordon of Earlston: "I wondered once at providence, and called white providence black and unjust, that I should be smothered in a town where no soul will take Christ off my hand. But providence hath another lustre with God than with my bleared eyes.... I see that infinite wisdom is the mother of His judgments, and that His ways pass finding out."[18]

A good illustration of Rutherford counseling friends to accept God's providence when events turned out contrary to what they had planned can be seen in the following incident. In 1636 John Stuart, provost of Ayr; Robert Blair; John Livingstone; and some other ministers, together with a considerable company of people set their hopes on traveling to New England to settle there. Because of extremely tempestuous weather, the ship they were sailing in had to turn back to Scotland. At the time, on hearing of this reverse, Rutherford

15. Rutherford to Viscountess Kenmure (letter 35), April 29, 1634, 97–98.

16. Samuel Rutherford, *Catechism, or The Sum of the Christian Religion* (Edinburgh: Blue Banner Productions, 1998), 20–21.

17. Rutherford to the Earl of Lothian (letter 83), 1637, 175; to David Dickson (letter 110), March 7, 1637, 226; and to William Dalgleish (letter 117), n.d., 238.

18. Rutherford to Alexander Gordon (letter 260), September 12, 1637, 510.

wrote to his friend Stuart: "I know it is no dumb providence, but a speaking one, whereby our Lord speaketh His mind to you, though, for the present ye do not well understand what He saith." Quoting Romans 8:28, "All things work together for good," he added, "ergo, shipwreck, losses, etc., work together for the good of them that love God." He saw such losses and disappointments and losses of friends as "God's workmen, set on work to work out good for you, out of everything that befalleth you."[19] Rutherford wrote to Robert Blair, believing him to have a submissive spirit, counseling him to be content in his present lot, saying, "Good is the will of the Lord, let it be done." He advised that God would bring mercy out of his sufferings and silence that grieved him at present.[20] Little did either of them know at that time that providence would soon bring them together to labor fruitfully together in St. Andrews for twenty years.

Looking back on this reverse a generation later, Robert Fleming, in recording the very stormy weather that forced their return to Scotland, referred to "truly a strange and remarkable providence, and their preservation in some kind miraculous." He added,

> Though it was very astonishing and bitter at the first look, yet was afterwards followed with a clear discovery from the Lord, as one of them with much freedom did express his assurance to the rest of his brethren, that since the Lord would not accept their service in America, they should not want work and service whither he was sending them back by so remarkable a providence, as within a short time was evident.[21]

Samuel Rutherford's contentment to let God work out His providential dealings and not seek to anticipate events is revealed in a letter to fellow minister in Galloway, William Dalgleish: "Providence hath a thousand keys, to open a thousand sundry doors for the deliverance of His own.... Let us be faithful, and care for our own part, which is to do and suffer for Him, and lay Christ's part on Him-

19. Rutherford to John Stuart (letter 161), 1637, 298–99.
20. Rutherford to Robert Blair (letter 89), February 7, 1637, 188.
21. Fleming, *Fulfilling of the Scripture*, 1:412–13.

self, and leave it there.... It is our part to let the Almighty exercise His own office, and steer His own helm."[22] This applied, he wrote a little later to Dalgleish regarding church affairs in general. God was in control, guiding events according to His good pleasure and infinite wisdom.[23]

The Importance of Prayer

In chapter 29 of his catechism on prayer, Rutherford asked first of all, "What is prayer?" Answer—"A humble incalling [invocation], upon God (Psalm 50:21), in faith (James 1:6) in the name of Christ (John 13:14), for all things that we need, either for our salvation or God's glory." To the following question about who should pray, he answered, "All are commanded to pray."[24]

As to when one should pray, Rutherford expressed his mind forcefully in his *Influences*. In opening up Psalm 57:7, he asked, "What shall beget a holy disposition to pray?" His answer: "Praying begets a holy disposition to pray." He then referred to David fleeing from Absalom (Psalm 3). As he fled he wept and prayed, "and that praying begets a fixedness to believe and a disposition to pray, as verse six shows, and a new disposition of assurance, verse 9." David's prayer in Psalm 6 was a prayer for mercy. That prayer was heard, and the result was a heavenly disposition to part with wicked men (v. 8) and a new disposition of assurance (v. 9).[25]

Rutherford maintained that dispositions to pray were various and changeable. That was the very time to pray for a quickening, for, he asks, "Why doth David pray so often to be quickened, if he was ever in a lively disposition?"[26]

Persistence in prayer was something he emphasized strongly. In preaching on the Syro-Phoenician woman, Rutherford said, "Afflictions drive us to seek God, they being God's firemen; and His hired

22. Rutherford to William Dalgleish (letter 117), 1637, 238.
23. Rutherford to Dalgleish (letter 197), 1637, 387.
24. Rutherford, *Catechism*, 64.
25. Rutherford, *Influences of the Life of Grace*, 287.
26. Rutherford, *Influences of the Life of Grace*, 242–43.

labourers, sent to break the clods, and to plough Christ's land, that he may sow heaven there." By contrast, "the prayers of the saints in prosperity, are but summer prayers, slow, lazy, and alas! too formal."[27] In a later sermon on Matthew 15:23, he brought out further the importance of persevering in prayer: "It is said, he answered her not a word; but it is not said he heard not one word: these two differ much. Christ often heareth when he doth not answer; his not answering is an answer, and speaks thus, Pray on, go on, and cry; for the Lord holdeth his door fast bolted, not to keep out, but that you may knock and knock."[28]

Rutherford believed in the value of prayer so much that he encouraged even those who were lacking in bodily strength or means to engage in prayer. In doing so, they would "set the whole wheels of Omnipotence on work," in which regard "the prayer of a sick and poor man shall do more in war for the cause of God, than twenty thousand men."[29] For "when God seemeth to sleep, in regard that his work and the wheels of his providence are at a stand, prayer awakeneth God, and putteth him on action."[30]

It was important to Rutherford that praying and believing should never be separated. This was brought out very clearly in a series of sermons on Matthew 9:27–31: "Praying with faith is like the breathings of a living man, that is hot and nourishes life, and keeps the body in a vital heat of life as long as it continues in the body."[31] He noted that both of the blind men prayed, and this prompted a reference to Matthew 18:19: "Again I say unto you, if two of you shall agree on earth as touching any thing that they shall ask, it shall be

27. Samuel Rutherford, *The Trial and Triumph of Faith* (Edinburgh: William Collins, 1845), 47–48.

28. Rutherford, *Trial and Triumph of Faith*, 115.

29. Rutherford, *Trial and Triumph of Faith*, 277.

30. Rutherford, *Trial and Triumph of Faith*, 273. He then refers to Psalm 44:23: "Awake, why sleepest thou, O Lord? Arise, cast us not off for ever."

31. Samuel Rutherford, *The Power of Faith and Prayer* (Stornoway: Reformation Press, 1991), 24. Originally published posthumously as *The Power and Prevalency of Faith and Prayer Evidenced in a Practical Discourse upon Matthew 9, 27–31.*

done for them of my Father which is in heaven."[32] Opposition, he pointed out (the multitude rebuking them, telling them to hold their peace) only "strengthened their crying in faith."[33] There were further spiritual ingredients in earnest prayer. There was vehemence of heart; therefore they cried. There was fervency of prayer in the Spirit. They were instant in prayer, crying by the way as they followed Christ. And there was praying with continuance, which "argues strong and heavenly desires without fainting."[34] They expressed their faith that Christ could heal them.[35]

The importance Rutherford attached to prayer can be seen in his response to a letter from John Fleming, bailie of Leith. Whether they knew each other from Rutherford's student days or not, this does illustrate the wide repute in which he was held. Fleming had asked him to draw up a Christian directory to assist him in his walk with God. Rutherford noted first that others had performed this task competently but agreed to offer his best services. Of the eight main points he made, the first four are on prayer. First, he advised that hours of the day should be given to the Word of God and prayer. Second, there should be time for ejaculatory prayer to God on spiritual and eternal matters, even in the midst of worldly employments. His third piece of advice was "to beware of wandering of heart in private prayers." Finally, there should be perseverance in prayer, even when one is in a downcast spirit.

As he did often with his correspondents, Rutherford laid bare his own soul, as it were, in his self-critical, self-effacing way, as he listed sixteen ways in which he felt he had been lacking in his own Christian life. His eleventh point was, on the one hand, that he had not wrestled in prayer as much as he ought to have done. On the other hand, he had been helped by giving time to prayer on journeys, by having days devoted to fasting and prayer, and in praying for others. He had been confirmed in the importance of prayer by answers

32. Rutherford, *Power of Faith and Prayer*, 24.
33. Rutherford, *Power of Faith and Prayer*, 26.
34. Rutherford, *Power of Faith and Prayer*, 40.
35. Rutherford, *Power of Faith and Prayer*, 46.

received, which encouraged him to persevere in prayer for all kinds of matters.[36]

In a similar vein he wrote to Marion McNaught to encourage her to continue in prayer for the cause of God and the oppressed kirk: "I testify and avouch it in my Lord, that the prayers ye sent to heaven these many years before are come up before the Lord, and shall not be forgotten."[37]

Rutherford urged persistent, importunate prayer on his correspondents. To Jean Gordon his advice was, "Give hours of the day to prayer. Fash [trouble] Christ (if I may speak so), and importune Him; be often at His gate; give His door no rest. I can tell you that He will be found."[38] In his last letter of several to Lady Culross, he urged continuance in prayer for a son "who is your grief," adding, "Your Lord waited on you and me, till we were ripe and brought us in." She was a deeply spiritual woman and a great encourager of the Lord's servants. She was one of a small group of people who prevailed in prayer the night before the awakening at Kirk of Shotts in 1630. She would no doubt respond positively to Rutherford's advice.[39]

As well as exhorting individuals to prayer, Samuel Rutherford felt, with other like-minded Presbyterians, that to reverse the spiritual declension and remove the innovations recently introduced, some measure of corporate prayer was called for. In a sermon at Anwoth in 1630 on Zechariah 13:7–9, he said, "An afflicted church is a praying church, and we need not be afraid of a praying church, if we could attain to this. If ye ask, why the Lord tries His children so hard? Answer, Because they are slack in prayer. God gets not that worship of prayer that is due to Him by fair means."[40]

While still at liberty at Anwoth, he was pleased to write to Viscountess Kenmure, announcing that there was a desire of "the best

---

36. Rutherford to John Fleming (letter 159), March 15, 1637, 292–95.

37. Rutherford to Marion McNaught (letter 221), July 8, 1637, 430.

38. Rutherford to Jean Gordon (letter 145), March 13, 1637, 275.

39. Rutherford to Lady Culross (letter 222), 1637, 433.

40. Samuel Rutherford, *Fourteen Communion Sermons*, 2nd ed. (1877; repr., Edinburgh: Blue Banner Productions, 1986), 44.

affected of the ministry" for a union of prayer "to cry to God with humiliation and fasting for the sins of the nation, for the lamentable and pitiful state of a glorious church," for the declension of too many in the ministry, "and the deadness of professors." Other matters for prayer included stirring up the nobles to take a stand for the Reformed faith and the prevalence of atheism and idolatry in the land.[41]

Three years later, Rutherford wrote from exile in Aberdeen to the Laird of Moncrieff, asking that he join with others of like mind in setting Wednesdays aside for prayer for the state of the kirk, adding, "We have no other armour in these evil times but prayer, now when the wrath from the Lord is gone out against this backsliding land."[42]

The continued importance of prayer to Rutherford can be seen in his last extant letter, in which he was continuing to stir up his contemporaries to give themselves to prayer. He called for families and private persons to engage in days of humiliation every month. He specified in his letter to John Murray, minister at Methven, various parts of the country that would be likely to respond positively to this, mentioning also certain other ministers, "to stir up one another that we may wrestle with the Lord for the remnant." He wrote as one "decaying most sensibly," yet on his deathbed looking to the Lord to "send a wakening among His own."[43]

Crosses—"Grace Withereth without Adversity"

In correspondence with John Fullerton in the parish of Borgue in Galloway, Rutherford commented on how difficult he found his exile in Aberdeen to begin with. He came to realize, however, the value of trials, or "temptations," as he called them: "I find it to be most

41. Rutherford to Viscountess Kenmure (letter 31), January 23, 1634, 92–93. The times agreed on were "the two first Sabbaths of February next, and the six days intervening betwixt these Sabbaths, as they may conveniently be had, and the first Sabbath of every quarter."

42. Rutherford to the Laird of Moncrieff (letter 171), March 14, 1637, 321.

43. Rutherford to John Murray (letter 365), n.d., 708.

true, that the greatest temptation out of hell is to live without temptations.... Grace withereth without adversity."[44]

In the first sermon of a short series on Jacob, "Fear Not, Thou Worm Jacob," Rutherford addressed the matter of crosses:

> Let us learn to take all our crosses from our (Lord) as it becomes us to do, and spill [mar, destroy] not our crosses by taking them from any other cause than the hand of God. If we could learn to put all our crosses over into our Lord's hand to be disposed of by Him, and to take them all from Him, we would get a better gate (way) of them nor (than) for the most part we do.[45]

The sermons were delivered in 1640 during the Bishops' Wars. They abound in reference to military affairs, for like other preachers in those days, Rutherford would often preach "to the times." His advice in the words that followed the above quotation was that his hearers should cast their *crosses*, *afflictions*, *trials*—words often found in his writings—on the Lord: "If all these things could be put over upon the Lord Himself by us, there is no doubt but He who is a giving and a pitying Lord, who sees our sufferings and our crosses, He would no doubt send a sure deliverance to such who, in faith and patience, commit themselves and all things that come upon them unto Him."[46]

To encourage his congregation to heed his exhortation, Rutherford presented three things that befell the Lord's people in their crosses that the world did not have. First, they would not be tested beyond what they could bear. Second, their crosses were "well watered over with the love and favour of God." Third, a point he often made in his correspondence, Christ shares in these sufferings: "And you should learn to make use of this and see when you are under crosses how sib [related] they are to Christ." He often used the word *halvers* to describe this.[47] He was well acquainted with

44. Rutherford to John Fullerton of Carleton (letter 157), March 14, 1637.
45. Rutherford, *Quaint Sermons*, 6.
46. Rutherford, *Quaint Sermons*, 6–7.
47. Rutherford, *Quaint Sermons*, 9–12.

one of his parishioners, Jonet Macculloch of the family of Ardwell near Anwoth. He had written to her in February 1637 to fasten her grip fast on Christ and have done with the world, feeling she needed some encouragement to go on for the Lord. Rutherford wrote again in September, advising that she cast her burden on the Lord and she would be sustained: "And then, let the wind blow out of what airth [direction] it will, your soul shall not be blown into the sea." He added, from his own experience, "I find Christ the most steadable [available] friend and companion in the world to me now. The need and usefulness of Christ are seen best in trials."[48]

Crosses, therefore, were to be expected. As Rutherford noted earlier in his letter to his parishioner Margaret Reid, crosses were determined before birth.[49] An afflicted life, he wrote to Marion McNaught, looked very much like the way to the kingdom.[50]

He elaborated on this point in a letter to Earlston, Younger: "For I am persuaded that it is a piece of the chief errand of our life…that we might suffer for a time here amongst our enemies; otherwise He might have made heaven to wait on us, at our coming out of the womb, and have carried us home to our country, without letting us set down our feet in this knotty and thorny life.… A piece of suffering, he concluded, "is carved to every one of us."[51] He reminded Viscountesss Kenmure that she could not have "a more pleasant or more easy condition here, than He had, who through afflictions was made perfect (Heb. 2:10)."[52]

Crosses were a means of refining one's faith, as he put it to Lady Robertland: "I find crosses Christ's carved work that He marketh out for us, and that with crosses He figureth and portrayeth us to His own image, cutting away pieces of our ill and corruption. Lord

---

48. Rutherford to Jonet Macculloch (letter 252), 1637, 496.

49. Rutherford to Margaret Reid (letter 248), n.d., 488. He made the point similarly in a letter to the wife of James Murray. Letter 304, n.d., 613.

50. Rutherford to Marion McNaught (letter 10), 1630, 50–51. His Scripture proofs for this statement were Acts 14:22; 1 Thessalonians 3:4.

51. Rutherford to Earlston, Younger (letter 196), 1637, 384.

52. Rutherford to Lady Kenmure (letter 11), June 26, 1630, 52.

cut, Lord carve, Lord wound, Lord do anything that may perfect Thy Father's image in us, and make us meet for glory."[53]

There is also a blessing that comes from crosses, which he noted to several of his correspondents. He described it to John Nevay, minister of Newmills, as the very element in which Christ's love lives.[54] To Earlston, Younger, he wrote that, contrary to what they intended, his enemies had contributed "to make me blessed."[55] To his close friend William Glendinning, provost of Kirkcudbright and a fellow sufferer for his beliefs at that time, Rutherford described his suffering in exile as "my garland and crown."[56]

By 1639 Rutherford would be laboring in St. Andrews with Robert Blair, who at that time was minister of the gospel at Ayr. In his capacity as a minister of the gospel there, Rutherford wrote:

> Suffering is the other side of our ministry, howbeit the hardest; for we would be content that our King Jesus should make an open proclamation, and cry down crosses, and cry up joy, gladness, ease, honour and peace. But it must not be so; through many afflictions we must enter into the kingdom of God. Not only by them, but through them, must we go; and wiles will not take us past the cross. It is folly to think to steal to heaven with a whole skin.[57]

---

53. Rutherford to Lady Robertland (letter 282), January 4, 1638, 547. He wrote likewise to the wife of the provost of Ayr: "I find no better use of suffering than that Christ's winnowing putteth chaff and corn in the saints to sundry places, and discovereth our dross from His gold, so as corruption and grace are so seen, that, Christ sayeth in the furnace, 'That is Mine, and this is thine.'" Letter 215, 1637, 422–23.

54. Rutherford to John Nevay (letter 179), June 15, 1637, 341.

55. Rutherford to Earlston, Younger (letter 271), 1637, 113.

56. Rutherford to William Glendinning (letter 212), July 6, 1637, 414.

57. Rutherford to Robert Blair (letter 89), February 7, 1637, 189.

6

Pastoral Advice to the Anwoth Flock

The correspondence of Samuel Rutherford reveals one possessed of great sympathy and tenderness in his dealings with his flock, to which he was devoted. He could reveal his inmost thoughts to them and to others further afield, never adopting a superior air, but speaking as one who was as indebted to the grace of God as others. He could also, as occasion demanded, use the language of stern rebuke in his desire to awaken those who were careless about their salvation.

After he had been in Aberdeen for several months, Rutherford wrote the first of two letters to his bereft flock on July 13, 1637.[1] Two months later a second, slightly shorter letter followed.[2] He also sent letters to individual members of his congregation. Many of the points raised in the two letters to his flock are included in letters not only to individual parishioners but also to those further afield in Scotland, in Ireland and England, with whom he was in touch.

Rutherford's parishioners were without a pastor at the time of his writing, which accounts for the anxiety he had for his flock, who were never far from his thoughts. His opening words, in fact, breathe his deep pastoral concern:

> I long exceedingly to know if the oft-spoken-of match betwixt you and Christ holdeth, and if ye follow on to know the Lord. My day-thoughts and my night-thoughts are of you: while ye sleep I am afraid of your souls, that they be off the rock. Next

1. Rutherford to his parishioners (letter 225), July 13, 1637, 438–44.
2. Rutherford to his parishioners (letter 269), September 23, 1637, 521–24.

> to my Lord Jesus and this fallen kirk, ye have the greatest share of my sorrow, and also of my joy; ye are the matter of the tears, care, fear, and daily prayers of an oppressed prisoner of Christ. As I am in bonds for my high and lofty One, my royal and princely Master, my Lord Jesus; so I am in bonds for you.[3]

He told them plainly of his "sad and heavy Sabbaths": "For, next to Christ, I had but one joy, the apple of the eye of my delights, to preach Christ my Lord; and they have violently plucked that away from me."[4] How he would be blessed if they were all Christ's: "Oh, how rich a prisoner were I, if I could obtain of my Lord (before whom I stand for you) the salvation of you all!... My witness is above; your heaven would be two heavens to me, and the salvation of you all as two salvations to me."[5]

Rutherford was adamant about one thing, that he had faithfully preached the truth of the Word of God to them. He emphasized this also in letters to several of his parishioners—for example, to Jonet Macculloch,[6] to Jean Macmillan,[7] to Cardoness, the Elder.[8] He also unburdened his fears to neighboring minister William Dalgleish: "If all that my Lord builded by me be casten down, and the bottom be fallen out of the profession of that parish, and none stand by Christ, whose love I once preached as clearly and plainly as I could...to that people; if so, how can I bear it?"[9]

In the meantime, what also greatly concerned him in his absence from his flock was that a hireling might enter in upon his labor. He often requested Marion McNaught's help to counsel others. In this

3. Rutherford to his parishioners (letter 225), July 13, 1637, 438.

4. Rutherford to his parishioners (letter 225), July 13, 1637, 438.

5. Rutherford to his parishioners (letter 225), July 13, 1637, 439.

6. Rutherford to Jonet Macculloch (letter 101), February 20, 1637, 211. "I persuade my soul that I delivered the truth of Christ to you. Slip not from it, for any bosts [threatened blows] or fears of men."

7. Rutherford to Jean Macmillan (letter 132), 1637, 259. "I told you Christ's testament and letter-will plainly, and I kept nothing back that my Lord gave me; and I gave Christ to you with good will."

8. Rutherford to Cardoness, the Elder (letter 166), 1637, 312.

9. Rutherford to William Dalgleish (letter 184), June 16, 1637, 359–60.

respect he wrote to her: "Pray, pray for my desolate flock, and give them your counsel, when you meet with any of them. It shall be my grief to hear that a wolf enter in upon my labours."[10]

With this danger in mind, Rutherford counseled his flock to "beware of the new and strange leaven of men's interventions, beside and against the word of God." He was referring to what he regarded as superstitious and idolatrous practices such as the Perth Articles had introduced. Above all, they should "forbear in any case to hear the reading of the new Fatherless Service-Book, full of gross heresies, popish and superstitious errors, without any warrant of Christ, *tending to the overthrow of preaching.*"[11]

In the various communications Rutherford received from Anwoth, one thing in particular distressed him greatly. He learned that in his absence many of his parishioners had gone back to their old ways. One of the evidences of this was misuse of the Sabbath. He reminded them of his first sermon among them on John 9:39.[12] His great desire as a preacher had been to help those who saw not to see the King and believe in Him, as He was proclaimed in the gospel. Now came a warning note: "I am ready to stand up as a preaching witness against such to their face, on that day, and to say 'Amen' to their condemnation, except they repent. The vengeance of the gospel is heavier than the vengeance of the Law."[13]

Rutherford could indeed be severe in his language when he deemed it necessary as he sought to admonish those who had sat under his ministry yet had gone back:

> I denounce eternal burning, hotter than Sodom's flames, upon the men that boil in filthy lusts of fornication, adultery, incest, and the like wickedness. No room, no, not a foot-breadth, for such vile dogs within the clean Jerusalem. Many of you put

10. Rutherford to Marion McNaught (letter 126), March 11, 1637, 250.

11. Rutherford to his parishioners (letter 225), July 13, 1637, 440; emphasis added.

12. "And Jesus said, For judgment I am come into this world, that they which see not might see; and that they which see might be made blind."

13. Rutherford to his parishioners (letter 225), July 13, 1637, 441.

> off all this with, "God forgive us, we know no better." I renew my old answer: the Judge is coming in flaming fire, with all his mighty angels, to render vengeance to all those that know not God, and believe not (2 Thess. 1, 8). I have often told you that security will slay you.[14]

As he looked back over his nine years at Anwoth with his parishioners, he was convinced there were some true believers in Christ among them. These he urged to give a large place in their households to Christ, to be exercised with prayer morning and evening. Serving the Lord, being faithful to Him, would bring its crosses, as he could well testify: "I am here one who hath some trial of Christ's cross, and I can say that Christ was ever kind to me, but He overcometh Himself (if I may speak so) in kindness while I suffer for Him. I give you my word for it, Christ's cross is not so evil as they call it; it is sweet, light, and comfortable."[15] His acceptance of his circumstances at that time would no doubt be an encouragement to them to remain faithful and to persevere in the faith.

By the time he wrote his second pastoral letter, Rutherford had been away from them for a year. He again expressed his concern for their spiritual state:

> My only joy out of heaven, is to hear that the seed of God sown among you is growing and coming to a harvest. For I ceased not, while I was among you, in season and out of season (according to the measure of grace given unto me), to warn and stir up your minds: and I am free from the blood of all men, for I have communicated to you the whole counsel of God.... Keep the truth of God, as I delivered it to you, before many witnesses, in the sight of God and His holy angels.[16]

He then returned to the innovations to be avoided, how the Lord's

14. Rutherford to his parishioners (letter 225), July 13, 1637, 442.
15. Rutherford to his parishioners (letter 225), July 13, 1637, 443.
16. Rutherford to his parishioners (letter 269), September 23, 1637, 521–22.

Supper should be observed, and keeping the Sabbath and no other special days.[17]

As noted in chapter 3, from Rutherford's earliest days in Anwoth he had set time aside to catechize his flock. On one occasion he had written to Marion McNaught of Kirkcudbright that he was presently going about catechizing those in his congregation.[18] In his absence, he exhorted his parishioners to use his catechism for their edification: "That ye should study to know God and His will, and to keep in mind the doctrine of the Catechism, which I taught you carefully, and speak of it in your houses, and in the fields, when ye lie down at night, and when ye rise in the morning; and that ye should believe in the Son of God, and obey His commandment."[19] It would appear that he had the words of Deuteronomy 6:4–7 very much on his mind here.

The absence of a pastor was something several congregations in Scotland were faced with in those days. Although he believed strongly in the primacy of preaching, Rutherford took a very realistic approach to this situation. When faced with this fact, how could a congregation be maintained spiritually? In his sermon "The Church Seeking Her Lord" (Song 5:7–10), he said, "The Word's working and the Spirit's working are not always confined to the hour of the sandglass, neither is the Spirit tied to a pulpit, and a gown, and a minister's tongue.... And often what ministers cannot do in public, God's Spirit with private helps will do it at home."[20] In his *Influences of the Life of Grace*, he wrote, "The meeting of believers for godly conference is owned by the Lord.... Nor is the acting of the Spirit tied only to public ministry; the saints take to their houses clusters of vine-grapes, which they fed upon at home. Let the saints meet, and by conference and prayer draw down new influences of the Spirit."[21]

How to continue when they did not have a gospel minister was one of the problems the congregation at Kilmalcolm in Renfrewshire

---

17. Rutherford to his parishioners (letter 269), September 23, 1637, 522.
18. Rutherford to Marion McNaught (letter 44), n.d., 113.
19. Rutherford to his parishioners (letter 269), September 23, 1637, 522–23.
20. Rutherford, *Quaint Sermons*, 124–25.
21. Rutherford, *Influences of the Life of Grace*, 307–8.

(123 miles by road from Anwoth today) put to him in one of their letters. His reply emphasizes the Word of God and how it can be used outside the walls of a church building:

> Remember that the Bible among you is the contract of marriage; and the manner of Christ's conveying His love to your heart is not so absolutely dependent upon even lively preaching, as that there is no conversion at all, no life of God, but that which is tied to a man's lips.... Make Christ your minister. He can woo a soul at a dykeside in the field. He needed not us, howbeit the flock be obliged to seek Him in the shepherd's tents.[22]

Rutherford ended his second pastoral letter with a further warning against any who took liberty to sin in his absence: "I here, under my hand, in the name of Christ my Lord, write to such persons all the plagues of God, and curses that ever I preached in the pulpit of Anwoth, against the children of disobedience!... And I shall stand up as a witness against you, if you do not amend your ways and your doings, and turn to the Lord with all your heart."[23]

He concluded his letter, however, in a much gentler, wooing tone by reminding them that he always had them in his heart:

> Alas! I could not make many of you fall in love with Christ, howbeit I endeavoured to speak much good of Him and to commend Him to you.... Yet, once again suffer me to exhort, beseech, and obtest [supplicate] you in the Lord, to think of His love, and to be delighted with Him, who is altogether lovely.... Ye are in my prayers night and day. I cannot forget you: I do not eat, I do not drink, but I pray for you all. I entreat you all and every one of you, to pray for me. Grace, grace be with you.[24]

---

22. Rutherford to the parishioners of Kilmalcolm (letter 286), August 5, 1638, 561. He was not long back from Aberdeen but took the time to answer several questions that they had.

23. Rutherford to his parishioners (letter 269), September 23, 1637, 523.

24. Rutherford to his parishioners (letter 269), September 23, 1637, 524.

7

Reasoning with Souls, Making Salvation Sure

From Samuel Rutherford's pastoral letters alone, it is clear that he believed there were many who had sat under his ministry and many further afield with whom he was in communication whose spiritual standing he was far from content with. Therefore, in his pastoral work at home in Anwoth, like in his letters, he was constantly seeking to correct wrong views of the way to salvation, the danger of false profession, and the importance of having a real conviction of sin. He was also at pains to ensure that his hearers loved not the world and had control of that master idol, self. The necessity of preparation for death and eternity was constantly urged on them, as they knew not what the future held.

Persevering with the Wayward

The spiritual progress of some of his correspondents can be traced more easily than others. Rutherford felt the need to persevere with some of his flock, particularly if they had been living in a way that gave no confidence there was spiritual life in them. One such was John Gordon of Cardoness, Elder, descended of the House of Gordon of Lochinvar. At the time of corresponding, Cardoness was an elderly man of strong passions that had led him astray in his earlier years. There is a tradition that at one time Cardoness was so incensed at the way Rutherford tackled him for exacting money from his tenants to pay for his castle expenses that he drove the pastor out of his home. He went for a time to worship at Kirkmabreck with William

Dalgleish.[1] This did not, however, seem to sever their relationship for good.

Rutherford indulged in plain talk with him:

> Dear Sir, I always saw nature mighty, lofty, heady, and strong in you; and that it was more for you to be mortified and dead to the world, than for another common man. Ye will take a low ebb, and a deep cut, and a long lance, to go to the bottom of your wounds in saving humiliation, to make you a won prey for Christ. Be humbled; walk softly.... Down, down, for God's sake, my dear and worthy brother, with your topsail. Stoop, Stoop! It is a low entry to go in at heaven's gate.... Come in, come in to Christ, and see what ye want, and find it in Him. He is the short (as we used to say), and the nearest way to an outgate [way of escape] of all your burdens. I dare avouch that ye shall be dearly welcome to Him; my soul would be glad to take part of the joy ye should have in Him.[2]

Rutherford was deeply concerned for the way Cardoness had lived without any sincere interest in the things of God; hence he stressed the need to humble himself and repent of his past life. He was nothing if not persevering in his pursuit of Cardoness's spiritual well-being, for a little later that same year he wrote again, this time also expressing concern for his family and his children: "Desire your children, in the morning of their life, to begin and seek the Lord, and to remember their Creator in the days of their youth (Eccles. xii, 1), to cleanse their way, by taking heed thereto, according to God's word (Ps.cxix, 9)."

He desired Cardoness also to share the thoughts of his letter to "others of my parishioners." He beseeched him, as one "now upon the very border of the other life," to cast himself and all his burdens on Christ: "Your Lord cannot be blamed for not giving you warning. I have taught the truth of Christ to you, and delivered unto you the

---

1. Alexander Whyte, *Samuel Rutherford and Some of His Correspondents* (Edinburgh: Oliphant, Anderson and Ferrier, 1904), 80–81; and Faith Cook, *Samuel Rutherford and His Friends* (Edinburgh: Banner of Truth, 1992), 42–43.

2. Rutherford to John Gordon of Cardoness, Elder (letter 82), 1637, 172–73.

whole counsel of God; and I have stood before the Lord for you, and I will yet still stand. Awake, awake to do righteously."[3]

He sent a third letter to Cardoness in June that year, again requesting that he show the people the content of his letter. This would mean reading it to those who were illiterate. Cardoness was on the edge of eternity: "And for yourself, I know that death is waiting, and hovering, and lingering at God's command. That ye may be prepared, then, ye had need to stir your time, and to take eternity and death to your riper advisement."[4]

Cardoness's pastor reminded him of how he had voiced his displeasure and dislike of his ways, both in public and private. He urged him to examine himself to see if he was in good earnest in Christ, bringing before him the example of apostates: "For some are partakers of the Holy ghost, and taste of the good word of God, and the powers of the life to come, and yet have no part in Christ at all. Many think they believe, but never tremble: the devils are farther on than these (James ii, 19). Make sure to yourself that ye are above ordinary professors."[5]

And there the record of the pleadings and exhortations of the "lawful and loving pastor"[6] ends. Did it achieve its end? In 1639 Cardoness was one of those who appended his signature to the unsuccessful petition of elders and parishioners seeking to keep Rutherford at Anwoth. This could indicate at least that his pastor's straight talking had not alienated him from his affections nor led to a rejection of his teaching entirely. There is also the evidence of one "Johnne Gordoun of Cardynes" signing the Minnigaff Covenant preserved in Cardonesss charter chest. If this is the one to whom Rutherford addressed his letters, perhaps this would indicate a change of heart? There is, last, the suggestion in one final brief letter that Cardoness had undergone a change of heart, for the pastor wrote, "Honourable, and dearest in the Lord—Your letter hath

3. Rutherford to Cardoness, Elder (letter 166), 1637, 310–11.
4. Rutherford to Cardoness, Elder (letter 180), June 16, 1637, 345.
5. Rutherford to Cardoness, Elder (letter 180), June 16, 1637, 346.
6. Rutherford to Cardoness, Elder (letter 180), June 16, 1637, 348.

refreshed my soul. My joy is fulfilled if Christ and ye be fast together. Ye are my joy and crown."[7] This would suggest that Cardoness was, at the least, not far from the kingdom of God.

John Gordon of Cardoness, Younger, followed his father into a life of debauchery and disregard for spiritual matters. He was deliberately offensive by his conduct on the Sabbath. He was unfaithful to his wife. Rutherford wrote to him from Aberdeen in response to a letter he had sent. In it he listed thirteen different reasons why he should seek salvation at once and ponder each of his pastor's points. The sad result of a Christless life was contrasted with the joy and peace of being in Christ's service. "Sin's joys are but night-dreams, thoughts, vapours, imaginations and shadows." Rutherford referred to the dignity of being a son of God and of having "dominion and mastery over temptations, over the world and sin." The pastor took time to commiserate with Cardoness and his wife for the loss of their children, using his oft-repeated phrase (where the words do vary slightly) that "they are not lost to you that are laid up in Christ's treasury in heaven."[8]

In a later letter, Rutherford warned Cardoness of the danger of continuing on in sin and hardening his heart: "And sinning against light will put out your candle, and stupefy your conscience, and bring upon it more coverings and skin, and less feeling and sense of guiltiness; and when that is done, the devil is like a mad horse, that hath broken his bridle, and runneth away with his rider whither he listeth—Learn to know that which the apostle knew, the deceitfulness of sin."[9]

Rutherford never gave up, even on those unresponsive to his pleas. He altered his approach slightly and besought Cardoness, Younger, to consider how his conscience was speaking to him, saying, "Why will ye die, and destroy yourself? I charge you in Christ's name, to rouse up your conscience, and begin to indent and con-

7. Rutherford to Cardoness, Elder (letter 124), n.d., 248.
8. Rutherford to John Gordon of Cardoness, Younger (letter 123), n.d., 247–48.
9. Rutherford to Cardoness, Younger (letter 199), 1637, 390–91.

tract with Christ in time, while salvation is in your offer." He further remonstrated with him to treat his wife with love and respect. Again, he presented to him the pleasures of the world as fleeting, ending by saying, "Take a trial of Christ. Look unto Him, and His love will so change you, that ye shall be taken with Him, and never choose to go from Him."[10]

Did he take a trial of Christ? Did he reform? In his introductory note to letter 123, Andrew Bonar made reference to an extant letter in the Wodrow manuscripts by Cardoness, Younger, couched in a religious tone, written to Thomas Wylie, minister of Borgue in the stewarty of Kirkcudbright. Cardoness wrote, "I entreat you be kind to my wife, and deal with her neither to take my absence, nor the form of coming from her, in evil part; for, in God's presence, public duties and nothing else removed me, or marred the form of my removal. Be earnest with her that she seek a nearer acquaintance with Christ: and fail not to pray for her and her family, and me."[11] It may well be that the words and prayers of Samuel Rutherford were instrumental in effecting a saving change in the life of Cardoness, Younger.

Awakening Those Secure in Their Morality

In his sermon "The Father's Welcome to the Forlorn Son" (Luke 15:20–21), Rutherford stated that there were two sorts of people who are hard to win for Christ. One sort he called "secure sinners," those who have no real apprehension of what God is or what heaven and hell are and continue on in their hardened, sinful ways.[12] Father and son Cardoness may be seen as falling into this category for much of their lives.

A second type of people is those who, still in a state of nature, "go under the name of honest men in the world"; these are individuals who had never descended into the depths of sin. Of such Rutherford said, "O! but it be a great matter to persuade such to fall in love with

10. Rutherford to Cardoness, Younger (letter 173), n.d., 324–25.
11. As quoted in the introduction to letter 123, 247.
12. Rutherford, *Quaint Sermons*, 254–55.

Christ, because they think they have as meikle [much] as to take them to heaven; and it is but a mistake when all is done. It is only nature that they take for grace. And there are thousands in the world who are beguiled with this." To his hearers he said very pointedly on this occasion that there were hundreds who listened to him, who believed they were going to heaven, but it was not so.[13] In another sermon at Anwoth, he said that many lived as if they had easy access to heaven: "Believe me, many men live as if they had the keys of heaven at their belt."[14]

In a 1634 Communion sermon at Anwoth on John 20:13–18, he contrasted the love and devotion of Mary Magdalene, who could not bear to be separated from Christ, with the weak profession of many of his hearers:

> We start all up to be professors! but few have the furniture for heaven. God forbid, that I should discourage any, but I see men contenting themselves with too little; some light, and weak love, to the word, and the preacher, and still their old sins and old jog-trot [slow and slovenly pace] is kept; and as dead in practice and reformation of life as they were ten years ago, and some of them worse. Now in the name and authority of the Son of God, try that it be good, sufficient work; see that it be stamped and sealed with Christ's arms.[15]

In his ministry, therefore, Samuel Rutherford labored much to bring his hearers and readers to the point of true repentance and faith in the Lord Jesus Christ. One of the marks of someone coming to faith in Christ was real conviction of sin. To one of his parishioners, Jean Macmillan, he expressed himself in this way:

> Salvation is not an easy thing, and soon gotten. I often told you that few are saved, and many damned: I pray you to make your poor soul sure of salvation, and the seeking of heaven your daily task. If ye never had a sick night and a pained soul for sin,

13. Rutherford, *Quaint Sermons*, 255.
14. Rutherford, *Fourteen Communion Sermons*, 197.
15. Rutherford, *Fourteen Communion Sermons*, 181.

> ye have not yet lighted upon Christ. Look to the right marks of having closed with Christ. If ye love Him better than the world, and would quit all the world for Him, then that saith the work is sound. Oh, if ye saw the beauty of Jesus, and smelled the fragrance of His love, you would run through fire and water to be at Him.[16]

Likewise to Margaret Ballantine, from outside Anwoth parish, he wrote in a similar strain of the need for true conviction of sin.[17]

John Bell, Elder, of Hentoun, once sat in a pew in Anwoth kirk. He added his name to the petition to keep Rutherford at Anwoth in 1639. Two years before this, Rutherford wrote with concern that he should be clear of the need for a renewed heart:

> Many are beguiled with this, that they are free of scandalous and crying abominations; but the tree that bringeth not forth good fruit is for the fire. The man that is not born again cannot enter into the kingdom of God. Common honesty will not take men to heaven. Alas! that men should think that ever they met with Christ, who had never a sick night, through the terrors of God in their souls, or a sore heart for sin!... I wish you an awakened soul, and that ye beguile not yourself in the matter of your salvation. My dear brother, search yourself with the candle of God, and try if the life of God and Christ be in you. Salvation is not casten to every man's door.[18]

Rutherford was continually challenging his correspondents as to the genuineness of their profession of faith. To Elizabeth Kennedy, sister of Hugh Kennedy, provost of Ayr, he wrote,

> I persuade myself that thousands shall be deceived and ashamed of their hope. Because they cast their anchor in sinking sands, they must lose it.... Oh, how many a poor professor's candle is

---

16. Rutherford to Jean Macmillan (letter 132), 1637, 259.

17. Rutherford to Margaret Ballantine (letter 79), 1637, 167–68. "I am sure that they never got Christ, who were not once sick at the yoke [onset] of the heart for Him. Too, too many whole souls think that they have met with Christ, who had never a wearied night for the want of Him."

18. Rutherford to John Bell, Elder (letter 218), 1637, 428.

> blown out, and never lighted again! I see that ordinary profession, and to be ranked amongst the children of God, and to have a name among men, is now thought good enough to carry professors to heaven.... I counsel you not to give your soul or Christ rest, nor your eyes sleep, till ye have gotten something that will bide the fire, and stand out the storm.[19]

"Mistaken grace, and somewhat like conversion which is not conversion, is the saddest and most doleful thing in the world. Make sure of salvation, and lay the foundation sure, for many are beguiled." This was his warning to parishioner William Halliday.[20] What Rutherford referred to as "the common faith and country-holiness, and week-day zeal" in a letter to Robert Brown of Carlsluth would never bring people to heaven. Therefore, he urged him, "Oh, Sir, turn, turn your heart to the other side of things, and get it once freed of these entanglements, to consider eternity, death, the clay bed, the grave, awesome judgment, everlasting burning quick in hell.... Consider heaven and glory."[21]

It did not matter to Samuel Rutherford how high people's standing in society might be, he faithfully exhorted them all to humble themselves and believe on the Lord Jesus Christ. The kingdom of God must be entered as a little child, he wrote to parishioner John Gordon, who made his home at Rusco Castle two miles from Anwoth: "Except ye receive the kingdom of God as a little child, and be as meek and sober-minded as a babe, ye cannot enter into the kingdom of God. That is a word which should touch you near, and make you stoop and cast yourself down, and make your great spirit

19. Rutherford to Elizabeth Kennedy (letter 87), 1637, 183–84.

20. Rutherford to William Halliday (letter 121), n.d., 245.

21. Rutherford to the Laird of Carsluth (letter 190), 1637, 374–76. In a similar vein, he besought John Lennox, Laird of Cally, "to give more pains and diligence to fetch heaven than the country sort of lazy professors, who think their own faith and their own godliness, because it is their own, best; and content themselves with a coldrife [heartless] custom and course." Letter 198, 1637, 388–89.

fall. I know that this will not be easily done, but I recommend it to you, as you tender your part of the kingdom of heaven."[22]

Rutherford urged his congregations to a spiritual importunity, never to give up seeking Christ when once begun. He realized, at the same time, that "we may preach unto you until our head rive [be rent] and our breasts burst; aye, we may preach unto you till doom's day, and yet that will not do the turn unless the inward calling of the Spirit be joined therewith." The outward call of the preacher must be accompanied by the inward drawing, as Christ Himself declared in John 6:44.[23]

Overcoming the Master Idol, Self

As Rutherford's hearers and readers sought the Lord, there were two areas of life they needed to gain mastery over and continue in once they were overcomers truly belonging to the Lord. These things loomed large also in Rutherford's assessment of himself. One was what he called "the master idol" and "this clay idol," self. The other was their relationship to the world. Rutherford did not stand apart from his correspondents in these things, but confessed his need to be continually attending to them, as one who had certainly not arrived: "Oh that I were free of that idol which they call myself; and that Christ were for myself; and myself a decourted [discarded] cypher, and a denied and forsworn thing!… Oh, but we have much need to be ransomed and redeemed by Christ from that master-tyrant, that cruel and lawless lord, ourself."[24] He saw self as the greatest thing to be conquered: "Oh, but we have need to be redeemed from ourselves, rather than from the devil and the world!"[25]

In his first letter to John Lennox, Laird of Cally, Rutherford expounded at some length on the master idol, self. Referring to

22. Rutherford to John Gordon (letter 147), 1637, 277–78.

23. Rutherford, "The Weeping Mary at the Sepulchre" (John 20:9–13), in *Quaint Sermons*, 71–72, 76. He preached this sermon in August 1640.

24. Rutherford to John Fergushill of Ochiltree (letter 188), 1637, 370.

25. Rutherford to the professors of Christ and His truth in Ireland (letter 284), February 4, 1638, 553–54.

several Scripture characters from Eve onward, including David and Solomon, he asked what made them fall into sin. The answer was that idol self, the old nature. Again, he did not stand apart from this but included himself in it: "Oh, blessed are they who can deny themselves, and put Christ in the room of themselves! Oh, would to the Lord that I had not a *myself*, but Christ; not a *my lust*, but Christ; nor a *my ease*, but Christ; nor a *my honour*, but Christ! O sweet word! '*I* live no more, but Christ liveth in me! (Gal. ii, 20).'"[26]

The personalizing of his words, putting himself into the frame, endeared him to his audience, encouraging them to accept his exhortations more readily. Bearing in mind also that many of his hearers were illiterate, the simple but vital emphasis on self would be something to which they could relate more easily.

The World a Passing Thing

In both his sermons and his correspondence, Rutherford was constantly seeking to woo his readers away from their attachment to the world. In a sermon on the Lamb's marriage (Rev. 19:7–14) preparatory to Communion, he addressed himself in marital terms to the need to forsake the world:

> If ye and the world be hand-fasted [contracted in marriage] together, that marriage must be divorced, or else He will not look on that side of the house that ye are in.... I suspect a hasty marriage to be a sudden vengeance; men and women fly to Christ, and flock to ordinances, to eat and drink with Him, ere ever He woo them. Many come to take Christ and have another husband at home, the world and your lusts. That is foul play: you must be single, or else ye cannot marry Him. I will ask at all of you that are come here this day, if your husband, the world, be dead? Try if your lusts be dead, and sin mortified; otherwise look for no match with Christ.[27]

26. Rutherford to the Laird of Cally (letter 198), 1637, 389–90.

27. Rutherford, *Fourteen Communion Sermons*, 294–95. Preached before the celebration of the Lord's Supper at Kirkcudbright, June 20, 1634.

In the same year in a preparation sermon before Communion at Kirkmabreck, he warned his hearers, "It is a dangerous thing once to let the world into the heart: if ye be in love with, and wedded to the world, then bid adieu to Christ."[28]

There was obviously a choice to be made, and there was no better illustration of this than the apostle Paul, who "weighed up all that the world had to offer, and is content to quit everything that he might gain Christ." This was the choice Rutherford's hearers must make: "If there come a competition between Christ and them, that we must either quit the one or the other."[29]

Those seeking the Lord needed to forsake the world, recognizing that it is of no lasting value to the Christian. Rutherford pressed home the worthlessness of the world even to those who were zealous Christians. Robert Gordon, bailie of Ayr, a cousin of Viscount Kenmure, and well established in local politics, was also a man of great piety and a keen supporter of the Presbyterian cause. He may, perhaps, have needed a bit of encouragement to have done with the world. Therefore Rutherford exhorted him, "But, alas! that that natural love which we have to this borrowed home that we were born in, and that this clay city, the vain earth, should have the largest share of our heart!" He went on to exhort him to condemn the world and turn his thoughts to Christ.[30] Alexander Gordon of Knockgray in the parish of Borgue (a neighbor to Anwoth), a zealous Covenanter who had entered into the blessings of salvation long before Rutherford, received the following advice, which epitomizes what he wrote with regard to this world, which was worthless:

There is nothing better than to esteem it our crucified idol (that is, dead and slain), as Paul did (Gal. vi, 14). Then let pleasures be crucified, and riches be crucified, and court and honour be crucified. And since the apostle saith that the world is crucified to him, we may put this world to the hanged man's doom, and to the gallows: and

28. Rutherford, *Fourteen Communion Sermons*, 77.

29. Rutherford, *Quaint Sermons*, 377–78.

30. Rutherford to Robert Gordon (letter 200), 1637, 393–94.

who will give much for a hanged man? as little should we give for a hanged and crucified world.[31]

There was always a sense of urgency in the ministry of Rutherford, whether in preaching or in writing. Life was uncertain in those days; the plague was still raging in various places. Several of his ministerial colleagues predeceased him. Therefore he would press on his audiences the need to seek the Lord while there was time, for they could not boast of tomorrow. He often used the hourglass as an illustration. To Margaret Ballantine he wrote, "For truly ye have need to make all haste, because the inch of your day that remaineth will quickly slip away; for whether we sleep or wake, our glass runneth.... My counsel to you is, that ye start in time to be after Christ; for if ye go quickly, Christ is not far from you.... I know this much of Christ, that He is not ill to be found, nor lordly of His love."[32] For John Lennox, Laird of Cally, he changed the metaphor: "Your sun, I know, is lower, and your evening sky and sunsetting nearer, than when I saw you last: strive to end your talk before night, and to make Christ *yourself*, and to acquaint your love and your heart with the Lord."[33]

All of his ministry, whether in the pulpit or in correspondence, demanded nothing less than the lordship of Christ. This was what true discipleship entailed. Writing to the Earl of Lothian, he highlighted one of the failings of many who would make a profession of being a follower of Christ (the earl himself was not included in these remarks): "but with a reservation that, by open proclamation, Christ would cry down crosses, and cry up fair weather, and a summer sky and sun, till we were all fairly landed at heaven."[34] Fair-weather Christians!

What he wrote to James Lindsay, a friend of Robert Blair and some other ministers, was applicable to both those who were seeking the Lord and others who were the Lord's but were tempted to backslide in their Christian lives: "But oh, how many of us would

---

31. Rutherford to Alexander Gordon (letter 223), 1637, 435.
32. Rutherford to Margaret Ballantine (letter 79), 1637, 166–68.
33. Rutherford to the Laird of Cally (letter 198), 1637, 390.
34. Rutherford to the Earl of Lothian (letter 83), 1637, 175.

have Christ divided into two halves, that we might take the half of Him only! We take His office, Jesus, and Salvation: but 'Lord' is a cumbersome word, and to obey and work out our own salvation, and to perfect holiness, is the cumbersome and stormy north-side of Christ, and that which we eschew and shift."[35] It would seem that the erroneous twenty-first-century error in some circles that teaches a person can have Jesus as Savior and not as Lord was something that ministers like Rutherford had to contend against in the early seventeenth century.

Although Rutherford placed great emphasis on making salvation sure for those who had truly found the Lord, he sought also to assure them of His keeping power and of the eternal security of each true believer. Two examples will suffice to conclude this chapter. In his sermon on the forlorn son, "He Was Lost and Is Found," Rutherford said, "There is no man who commits himself unto Christ, who ventures his life and all for Christ's cause and for religion, [but] He will answer for all that are given to Him. And when He renders up the kingdom to His Father, He will make such compt [account] of them as that which we read, John xvii.12, where He says: 'Of all that Thou hast given Me have I lost none, but the child of perdition; that the Scripture might be fulfilled.'"[36]

In a sermon on Isaiah 49:1–4 preached at a Communion at Kirkmabreck on July 19, 1634, he encouraged his hearers with these words: "If ye truly believe in Him as He is offered to you in the everlasting gospel, there is no fear that He cast you off or that ye shall not be saved. Whom He loves, He loves unto the end. If ye are His, He will not lose His right. Then boldly claim salvation, forgiveness, and Christ's righteousness. It is yours by God's calling; take your own and be not driven from it."[37]

---

35. Rutherford to James Lindsay (letter 234), September 7, 1637, 467.
36. Rutherford, *Quaint Sermons*, 298.
37. Rutherford, *Fourteen Communion Sermons*, 119.

8

The Need for Sanctification and Mortification

Rutherford wrote to James Lindsay, "Sanctification and mortification of our lusts are the hardest part of Christianity."[1]

At the Westminster Assembly, the delegates spent much time reaching agreement on several parts of the Confession of Faith, especially in debating the eternal decree. The Confession of Faith has been described as "a triumph for the Scottish supralapsarian school of theology."[2] Samuel Rutherford played a large part in these proceedings. Chapter 13, "Of Sanctification," states:

> They who are once effectually called, and regenerated, having a new heart, and a new spirit created in them, are further sanctified, really and personally through the virtue of Christ's death and resurrection, by His word and Spirit dwelling in them: the dominion of the whole body of sin is destroyed, and the several lusts thereof are more and more weakened and mortified.... This sanctification is throughout, in the whole man; yet imperfect in this life, there abiding still some remnants of corruption in every part; whence ariseth a continual and irreconcilable war, the flesh lusting against the Spirit, and the Spirit against the flesh.[3]

---

1. Rutherford to James Lindsay (letter 234), September 7, 1637, 467.

2. Rendell, *Samuel Rutherford*, 68.

3. *Westminster Confession of Faith* (Glasgow: Free Presbyterian Publications, 1973), 61–62. The Shorter Catechism is more succinct: "Question 35, What is sanctification? Answer: Sanctification is the work of God's free grace, whereby we are renewed in the whole man after the image of God, and are enabled more and more to die unto sin, and live unto righteousness." *Westminster Confession of Faith*, 297.

In his own catechism, designed for the use of his rural flock, many of the people with limited or no education, Rutherford put it more simply in chapter 23: "Question, what is sanctification? Answer, It is the work of God's Spirit by the Word putting in us the life of Christ and renewing all the powers of our soul." He then asked, "What are the parts of sanctification? Answer, In removing of the stony heart and slaying of sin, and a quickening of us to love righteousness (Ezekiel 36, 26–27)." Sanctification was a matter in which justified individuals were essentially active. Their working out of their salvation was evidence that God was working in them.

Rutherford spelled out the way to make progress in sanctification in his *Influences of the Life of Grace*. He described it in terms of "heavenly" dispositions in the affections of the soul. These consisted of the following five things. First, believers must give themselves to the study of the Word and meditate on the promises. King David was the example of this as one who learned, observed, and loved the testimonies. Second, a person should be much in prayer, attending to the Word and conferring with others about the Scriptures. A third essential was to put into practice the exhortation of Colossians 3:1–3, recognizing that one has risen with Christ and should set the affections on heavenly things. Fourth, the believer should be sensitive to the Holy Spirit's leading and guiding, seeking to avoid grieving and quenching the Spirit. Last, one should avoid quenching guidance being given and let the conscience speak. That way, wrote Rutherford, "you will get divine dispositions and suitable influences."[4]

Mortification, putting to death all that would hinder growth in grace and the knowledge of the Lord, loomed large in Rutherford's thinking. In his *Covenant of Life Opened*, he asked, "What is Mortification?" His answer: "It is a deadening of the whole powers and inclinations of the soul in their bentnesse and operations, in order to things forbidden by the Law of God, or in things indifferent and commanded. Hence, not the affections only, but the understanding and mind must be deadened. And therefore this is no mortification

4. Rutherford, *Influences of the Life of Grace*, 301–2.

until sin original be subdued in its damnation by Christ's death, and in its dominion by the Spirit of Sanctification."[5]

He proceeded in the next twenty pages to develop this definition. He posed another question—"To what things must we be crucified?" His answer, based on Galatians 2:14, is, "To all things created, to the world; we condemn and despise and hate the world, and the world does value us nothing."[6]

As noted earlier, Rutherford often included his own experience in correspondence to his parishioners and others. As he observed his own spiritual growth, in spite of the tenacity of the old nature in him, he questioned which was the greater reason for Christ to be loved—for giving sanctification or free justification? He put it in this way to Robert Gordon of Knockbreck: "And I hold that he is more and most to be loved for sanctification. It is in some respect greater love in Him to sanctify, than to justify; for He maketh us most like Himself in His own essential portraiture, and image, in sanctifying us.... I think sanctification cannot be bought: it is above price. God be thanked for ever, that Christ was a told-down [above] price for sanctification."[7]

As Rutherford observed Christian society around him, he felt there were few taking the matter of sanctification with due seriousness: "We say that we are removing and going from this world; but our heart stirreth not one foot off its seat. Alas! I see few heavenly minded souls, that have nothing upon the earth but their body of clay going up and down this earth, because their soul and the powers of it are up in heaven, and there their hearts live, desire, enjoy, rejoice."[8]

The primacy of sanctification in Rutherford's mind can be seen in his advice to the son of an old friend. John Meine Jr., whose father, John Meine the merchant, had been an influence for good to Rutherford during his student days in Edinburgh, was preparing himself for the ministry. To the young man Rutherford gave timely advice, no

---

5. Samuel Rutherford, *The Covenant of Life Opened, or, A Treatise of the Covenant of Grace* (Edinburgh: Andrew Anderson, 1655), 261.

6. Rutherford, *Covenant of Life Opened*, 268.

7. Rutherford to Robert Gordon (letter 170), 1637, 320–21.

8. Rutherford to Robert Lennox (letter 213), 1637, 416–17.

doubt with a text like 1 Timothy 4:16[9] in mind: "If ye would be a deep divine, I recommend to you sanctification."[10] He gave no advice, for example, about methods of study. He followed it up, however, in a second letter in reply to a further communication, in which he spoke of the immutability of Christ, even when His own are changeable. As he told young Meine to fear backsliding, he continued: "I had stood sure if I had, in my youth, borrowed Christ to be my bottom. But he that beareth his own weight to heaven shall not fail to slip and sink."[11]

Rutherford was very conscious that many people attended ordinances "for the fashion."[12] Therefore he was at pains at Communion services to emphasize that those present be in a right spiritual state to partake. In a sermon preparatory to Communion at Kirkmabreck in 1634 on Luke 14:16–24, the response of those invited to the great supper, he said, "This should teach us to strive for mortification; for when the apostle speaks of this sin, the lust of the flesh, that which is to be done against it is, that it should be taken to the cross and crucified. The eyes, the ears and the heart of the old man must be nailed to Christ's cross. We shall never get the victory over this temptation except we be dead men to the world."[13]

Likewise, in another preparatory sermon at Kirkmabreck on Hebrews 12:1–5 under the heading "Cast off the sin that doth so easily beset us," he urged his hearers to be actively "hacking, and cutting the branches, and roots" of remaining corruption in their lives.[14]

---

9. "Take heed unto thyself, and unto the doctrine; continue in them: for in doing this thou shalt both save thyself, and them that hear thee."

10. Rutherford to John Meine Jr. (letter 81), January 5, 1637, 170.

11. Rutherford to John Meine Jr. (letter 240), September 7, 1637, 476–77. Meine would later be inducted as minister of Anwoth.

12. Rutherford, *Fourteen Communion Sermons*, 199.

13. Rutherford, *Fourteen Communion Sermons*, 81.

14. Rutherford, *Fourteen Communion Sermons*, 96–97.

> This is the body of sin that remains in our nature; he speaks of it, as if one had us clasped in his arms. For original sin has us in fetters as captives.... The dominion of it we break by grace. Every woe [sore] heart we have, for this indwelling sin, breaks a bone of old Adam, gives him back a crack, and makes him cry. As we repent, and advance in holiness, we break a leg, or an arm of this sin; but for the root of it, God only, in death can pluck it out. Yet we must be

In an earlier letter to Robert Gordon of Knockbreck, Rutherford wrote that he was aware that mortification and being crucified to the world was "not so highly accounted of by us as it should be." From his exile in Aberdeen, however, he could write of himself: "I scarce now either hear or see what it is that this world offereth me.... One night of what my Lord hath let me see within this short time is worth a world of worlds." The phrase "within this short time" refers to his time in Aberdeen, where he was himself growing in grace, having followed after holiness in earnest.[15]

Exhorting to Make Progress in Sanctification

One of the Campbells of Argyll, Lady Jane Kenmure, was a deeply spiritual woman who, nevertheless, had several crosses to bear in her life. She did not enjoy the best of health, being subject to periods of depression. Alexander Whyte noted that "her whole life was drenched with a deep melancholy."[16] She had made what many regarded as an ill-advised marriage to Sir John Gordon of Lochinvar in 1628. (The subject of his deathbed restoration will be covered later.) Three daughters from this marriage died in infancy, which drew forth letters of consolation from Rutherford.[17] A son by the same marriage, John, second Viscount Kenmure, predeceased her in 1639. A second, more congenial marriage to Sir Henry Montgomery of Giffen lasted only a few years, there being no children from that union.

In a letter to her in January 1632, Rutherford referred to harping again on a common string: "that there is a necessity of advancing in the way to the Kingdom of God, of the contempt of the world, of denying ourself and bearing our Lord's cross, which is no less needful for us than daily food." He said that the sure mark that she was on

---

hacking, and cutting the branches, and root of it, else we cannot make progress in our race. We must not take this defiling sin forward with us in our race.... We must leave it when we start, and deliver it over to Christ, that He may put it on His cross, and nail it to His gallows.

15. Rutherford to Robert Gordon (letter 92), February 9, 1637, 196.

16. Whyte, *Samuel Rutherford and Some of His Correspondents*, 29.

17. Rutherford to Lady Kenmure (letter 4), January 15, 1629, 41; letter 30, November 15, 1633, 90; and letter 35, 1637, 97–98.

course for heaven was how the love of God filled her heart, and she had no care for earthly things: "By this, Madam, ye know, ye have betrothed your soul in marriage to Christ, when ye do make but small reckoning of all other suitors or wooers."[18] The following month he was exhorting her to keep her first love: "There is none like Him; I would not exchange one smile of His lovely face with kingdoms."[19] The next year he noted with confidence that she was going forward in her spiritual journey. He was mindful, however, of the dangers she was exposed to because of her high status in society, "higher than the rest," with the possibility of succumbing to vainglory.[20]

From his exile in Aberdeen, Rutherford exhorted the viscountess to keep herself in the love of Christ "and stand back from the pollutions of the world."[21] After more than two decades of correspondence, he could write to Viscountess Kenmure, confident that she had experienced mercies, deliverances, plenty of means, consolations, manifestations of God, "by all which, ye may be comforted now, and confirmed in the certain hope, that grace, free grace, in a fixed and established Surety, shall perfect that good work in you."[22]

---

18. Rutherford to Lady Kenmure (letter 21), January 14, 1632, 72.
19. Rutherford to Lady Kenmure (letter 23), February 13, 1632, 78.
20. Rutherford to Lady Kenmure (letter 30), November 15, 1633, 90–91.
21. Rutherford to Lady Kenmure (letter 94), 1637, 199.
22. Rutherford to Lady Kenmure (letter 341), May 27, 1658, 674.

9

Counseling Some Who Had Doubts

In an article in *The Month* magazine, J. M. Ross pointed out that if Rutherford was not forthcoming with a lot of advice on conduct, he was definitely unsparing in his counsel on the spiritual life. In particular, he was forthcoming and very helpful to those who perhaps could not point to a date when they became Christians or lacked assurance of forgiveness for past sins or even felt the absence of Christ.[1]

In chapter 31 of his catechism, "Of the Certainty of Our Salvation," Rutherford asked, What grounds of assurance of salvation are in God? The answer—God has decreed to save us; we have God's power, His promise and covenant, and oath, and Christ prays for us that our faith fail not.[2] He then asked what warrants we have within us. Answer—His Spirit dwelling in us to the end. His Spirit witnesses with our spirit that we are God's sons and heirs.[3] This was followed by a question that many in those days would have asked: But may we not then sleep and fold our hands and commit all the care of God to our salvation? His answer—It is a work of God's Spirit and a sure means of our continuance that God by His Spirit makes us careful to work out our salvation in fear and trembling. He asked a further question: What is the witnessing of our spirit? Answer—It is the knowledge and feeling that my renewed mind and heart has of God's unchangeable love to me in Christ. He then asked, What is it

---

1. J. M. Ross, "The Salient Features of Rutherford's Spirituality," *The Month, A Review of Christian Thought and World Affairs* (July 1975): 209–10.

2. Rutherford, *Catechism*, 69.

3. Rutherford, *Catechism*, 69–70.

then to receive earnest of God and to be filled by the Spirit of promise unto the day of redemption? Answer—When God has given me the graces of His Spirit as an earnest penny that I shall receive glory, and my soul is as a sealed and closed letter, stamped with the image of Christ with all the power thereof.[4]

In another of his works, *Examen Arminianismi*, he wrote, "Indeed, the certainty of salvation, according to the word of God, is as absolute and certain…as is the promise of God that he would not cover the earth again with the waters of Noah, Isa. 54.9–10, and as is the faithful covenant of God with respect to the succession of the nights and the days, and the movements of the Sun and the Moon, Jer. 31. 35–6."[5]

In Rutherford's pastoral work, there were always those whose salvation he did not doubt, and those he believed were far from salvation. There was also, however, a small minority of professing Christians who had their own personal doubts. One such was his parishioner John Clark. He had approached Rutherford, it would seem, feeling somewhat isolated and unsure of his standing. Rutherford's letter in reply began by stressing the need for perseverance. Then, having 2 Corinthians 13:5[6] very much in mind, Rutherford provided Clark with nine marks of a true Christian that a reprobate would not have. He could then assess his own standing in the light of these marks. Foremost was love for Christ, which should keep him from sinning. His possession of Christ should show itself in self-abnegation, good works, a life guided by the Word of God in all things. An essential mark, also, was daily praying and supplication with thanksgiving. It was essential also, Rutherford believed, to hold fast to what he had taught him "and have nothing to do with the corruptions and new guises entered into the house of God." He was referring to the "innovations" he condemned repeatedly in his correspondence.[7]

---

4. Rutherford, *Catechism*, 70–71.

5. As quoted in Richard, *Supremacy of God*, 210.

6. "Examine yourselves, whether ye be in the faith; prove your own selves. Know ye not your own selves, how that Jesus Christ is in you, except ye be reprobates?"

7. Rutherford to John Clark (letter 172), n.d., 324.

Only one letter to William Gordon of Kenmure is extant.[8] He had written to Rutherford because he was concerned that he was doubting his standing in Christ. Rutherford first pointed him to one of the "we knows" of John's first epistle: "We know that we have passed from death unto life, because we love the brethren" (3:14). More Scripture proofs, he wrote, would follow. Gordon was complaining of deadness and of remaining sin in his life. Rutherford saw this as a sign of spiritual life in him: "the more pain, and the more night-watching, and the more fever, the better." Where Gordon went wrong was in thinking that lack of victory suggested he had no grace. To this Rutherford replied, "Nay, say I, the want of *fighting* were a mark of no grace; but I shall not say the want of *victory* is such a mark...for there is great odds between doubting that we have grace, and trying if we have grace. The former may be sin, but the latter is good. We are but loose in trying our free holding of Christ, and making sure work of Christ." He urged Gordon to examine himself on a regular basis: "Each man had need twice a-day, and oftener, to be riped [examined], and searched with candles." If he did this, he would then be in a much healthier state than those professors who never seek to make their calling and election sure.[9] This latter point was always a great emphasis in the pastor's reasoning.

James Bautie (or Beattie) was another correspondent who had doubts, even though he seems to have been preparing for the ministry. He was obviously one given to serious introspection, something Rutherford could relate to. He had made the mistake of comparing himself with more mature Christians who had made more progress in spiritual things. Rutherford responded by saying that "even the best regenerate souls have their defilements and carnality." Another problem he had was that sometimes he seemed to have more

8. Bonar suggests that he may be the William Gordon of Roberton in the parish of Borgue in Galloway and that he may have been on a visit to Kenmure. Introduction to letter 72, 153.

9. Rutherford to William Gordon (letter 203), 1637, 400–401. "For I see many leaky vessels fair before the wind, and professors who take their conversion upon trust, and they go on securely, and see not the under-water, till a storm sink them."

fervency in prayer with his neighbor than when he was by himself. He wondered if this was due to hypocrisy on his part. To this Rutherford replied, "If this be always, no question a spice of hypocrisy is in it, which should be taken heed to. But possibly desertion may be in private, and presence in public, and then the case is clear."[10]

Another problem Bautie had, something Rutherford himself was familiar with, was Christ's short visits to him. The pastor was full of sympathy here, being acquainted with Christ's visits and withdrawings. His advice was to treat the Lord well, "give Him the chair and the boardhead [head of the dinner table], and make Him welcome to the mean portion ye have. A good supper and kind entertainment maketh guests love the inn the better." He continued by pointing out that Christ sometimes withdraws for the purpose of trying the soul and so goes away elsewhere for a time.[11] Writing on this subject in his *Influences of the Life of Grace*, Rutherford said, "Withdrawings of Christ teach to try whether we have abused his manifestations formerly." In such a case, "the spouse then under the withdrawing of Christ [referring here to Song 5:6], is here put to see her poverty and speak by others her case to Christ, when she neglected to speak to Christ when He was nearer to her than now."[12]

Shortly after he had settled in St. Andrews, having just been appointed professor of divinity at the New College, Rutherford, though pressed for time, took time to reply to a letter from James Wilson. This correspondent's exact family connections and location are uncertain. He was obviously someone exercised in his own soul, having given deep thought to his standing in Christ. Rutherford opened by pointing out that the Lord so cared for His new creation that He was "going over it again, and trying every piece in you, and blowing away the motes of His new work in you." Wilson's very questions "Am I His?" and "Whose am I?" suggested that he belonged to the Lord. Therefore, Rutherford replied, "I charge you by the mercies

10. Rutherford to James Bautie (letter 249), 1637, 492.
11. Rutherford to James Bautie (letter 249), 1637, 489–94.
12. Rutherford, *Influences of the Life of Grace,* 310–11.

of God, be not that cruel to grace and the new birth as to cast water on your own coal by misbelief." He urged Wilson to give Christ time to work in his heart: "Hold on in feeling and bewailing your hardness; for that is softness to feel hardness." Above all he should bid the Holy Spirit to "do His office in you." He reminded Wilson that faith was one thing, and the feeling and notice of faith another.[13]

That same year, Lady Fingask wrote to Rutherford with apparent misgivings about her spiritual standing. In reply he said that unbelief was a spiritual sin "and so not seen by nature's light; and that all which conscience saith is not Scripture." From his own experience he could testify as to how sins of his youth returned to haunt him. He counseled her to look outside herself to the unchanging Christ, who loved her before the creation of the world: "He cannot change His mind; because He is God, and resteth in His love." He ended by saying, "True faith is humble, and seeth no way to escape but only in Christ. And I believe that ye have put an esteem and high price upon Christ."[14]

---

13. Rutherford to James Wilson (letter 293), January 8, 1640, 588–91.
14. Rutherford to Lady Fingask (letter 297), March 27, 1640, 600–602.

10

Pastoral Concern for Children and Youth

Samuel Rutherford had a great love for children. In his correspondence he often devoted a few sentences or a paragraph of a letter with the spiritual welfare of children in mind. His regular communication with Marion McNaught, whose counsel he valued very much, enables us to trace the progress of her children, which may represent other family interests that he had. In his first letter, he expressed a prayerful interest in the whole family: her husband, William Fullerton, provost of Kirkcudbright; and their two sons, William and Samuel.

Rutherford also had a particular interest in their daughter, Grizzel. Already he had spoken with her and was "in good hopes that the seed of God is in her, as in one born of God." He promised her mother he would bear her up before the throne of grace, cautioning her: "I trust you will acquaint her with good company, and be diligent to know with whom she loveth to haunt."[1] Three years later, Grizzel was longing for a Bible.[2] Rutherford's prayerful interest in all of Marion McNaught's children was expressed at the end of a letter in May 1631: "God shall give you joy of your children. I pray for them by their names. I bless you from our Lord, your husband and children."[3]

The language he used later that year suggests that the children of the family were growing up and were able to take on more responsibility for their own conduct: "I pray for you, with my whole soul and desire, that your children may walk in the truth, and that the Lord

1. Rutherford to Marion McNaught (letter 1), June 6, 1627, 33.
2. Rutherford to Marion McNaught (letter 10), 1630, 51.
3. Rutherford to Marion McNaught (letter 14), May 7, 1631, 60.

may shine upon them, and make their faces to shine, when the faces of others shall blush. I dare promise them, in His name, whose truth I preach, if they will but try God's service, that they shall find Him the sweetest Master that ever they served."[4]

He noted to McNaught that Christ was unknown to the young ones. They do not seek Him because they do not know Him. He urged them, therefore, to try for a while the service of this blessed Master. He ended by entreating them "in Christ's name to try what truth and reality is in what I say, and leave not His service till they have found me a liar."[5] His wishes for them shortly after were that they would be "corner-stones in Jerusalem," once they were united to the "fair Chief Corner-stone."[6] The following year found him entreating them to covenant with Jesus Christ to be His, "that they may have acquaintance in heaven, and a friend at God's right hand."[7]

It was not just Grizzel about whom Rutherford was prayerfully concerned.[8] He noted that one of McNaught's sons had entered school. Rutherford's closeness to the family is clear in a letter in which he promised to do the best he could to help him if McNaught was called home, "every way in grace and learning, and his brothers, and all your children. And I hope that you would expect that of me." He concluded his letter by praying that while these children were "green and young," they commit their lives to the Lord.[9]

Rutherford valued so greatly the prayers of the Lord's people for children that he brought their needs before other colleagues and correspondents. For example, in a letter to Viscountess Kenmure, who had the misfortune of losing children in 1629 and 1634, he informed her that he had been in touch with others, asking them to bear up in prayer her child who was sick at that time. Several people had been

4. Rutherford to Marion McNaught (letter 16), n.d., 63–64.
5. Rutherford to Marion McNaught (letter 16), 1631, 63–64.
6. Rutherford to Marion McNaught (letter 18), n.d., 66–67.
7. Rutherford to Marion McNaught (letter 24), March 9, 1632, 82.
8. Rutherford to Marion McNaught (letter 34), April 25, 1634, 96–97.
9. Rutherford to Marion McNaught (letter 46), 1634, 115–16.

contacted for this purpose, including Andrew Cant, James Martin, and the Lady Leyes.[10]

Avoiding the Follies of Youth

Rutherford's concern for youth is expressed in many of his letters. It is also the subject of some of his sermons. He was fond of doing short series of sermons on certain passages of Scripture. One of these was on what he called the "forlorn son" of Luke 15. In a sermon on Luke 15:11–12, he asked, "Why is it that he gives him who leaves his father the style of the younger son?" His answer: "To tell us that it is a trick of youth for any to leave Christ, that it is an ordinary thing for young ones to tire of God's company, and to long to be at their own tutoring." He gave three reasons why youth are prone to fall. First, because those who are young have no experience. He made reference to Psalm 119:9,[11] believing this passage was in Scripture to warn that "it is a question, and hard, for a young man to hold his feet and hear what God says to him." A second reason: "While the lusting of youth is strong, it is hard to serve God." Third, he wrote, "While there is no time of our age that is meet for God in itself…the most unmeet [unfit] time of all is the time of our youth."[12]

As he penned the following words, was he reflecting on the sins of his own youth, about which he was never explicit?

> O! that young ones would start to in time to seek the Lord while they are young, that they would begin to make their acquaintance with the Lord and to drink in the knowledge of the Son of God, that they would study to know the sweetness of His love, that they would set to get their young hearts married on Christ! If they will do so once, give Him their love, and their hearts' love, it shall not be in their power to follow another lover again.[13]

---

10. Rutherford to Lady Kenmure (letter 206), June 17, 1637, 406.

11. "Wherewithal shall a young man cleanse his way? by taking heed thereto according to thy word."

12. Rutherford, *Quaint Sermons*, 207–9.

13. Rutherford, *Quaint Sermons*, 209.

It was noted earlier that John Gordon of Cardoness, Younger, was one who had followed his father's bad example. To him Rutherford wrote as pastor of what a dangerous time youth was:

> It is not possible for you to know, till experience teach you, how dangerous a time youth is. It is like green and wet timber. When Christ casteth fire on it, it taketh not fire. There is need here for more than ordinary pains, for corrupt nature hath a good back-friend of youth.... Learn to know that which the apostle knew, the deceitfulness of sin. Struggle to make prayer, and reading, and holy company, and holy conference your delight.[14]

Rutherford's concern for the young showed itself also in the way that he sought to persuade young people, even from the most godly of households, to seek the Lord. For example, he continued to express his concern for Grizzel as she grew up, urging her to give herself to Christ and to get seriously acquainted with the Scriptures and the promises found therein. He charged her to fulfill her mother's joy "and learn Christ, and walk in Christ.... Let her begin at prayer; for if she remember her Creator in the days of her youth, He will claim kindness to her in old age." He assured the mother of his continued prayers in this regard.[15]

Concern for Grizzel was again evident in two letters the following year.[16] Three years later, Rutherford pointed Grizzel to the example of her godly mother, adding, "You are the seed of the faithful, and born within the covenant; claim your right. I would not exchange Christ Jesus for ten worlds of glory.... I recommend Him to you above all things."[17] As late as 1653, he was exhorting her to follow Christ fully when others were cold. By this time her mother had been in heaven for ten years. Referring to how her mother had "quickened many about her to the seeking of God," he desired to continue on in the

---

14. Rutherford to John Gordon of Cardoness, Younger (letter 199), 1637, 390–91.

15. Rutherford to Marion McNaught (letter 41), 1634, 107–8.

16. Rutherford to Marion McNaught (letter 50), April 22, 1635, 123; and letter 51, 1635, 124.

17. Rutherford to Grizzel Fullerton (letter 155), March 14, 1637, 286–87.

same way "and be letting a word fall to your brethren and others, that may encourage them to look toward the way of God."[18]

When he heard of young people who had begun to follow the Lord, Samuel Rutherford was not short with praise and further encouragement. He rejoiced to hear from William Livingstone, most likely one of his parishioners, how he was "so early in the morning matched with such a Lord; for a young man is often a dressed lodging for the devil to dwell in." Rutherford recommended him, however, to give attention to prayer and watching over the sins of youth, for "Satan hath a friend at court in the heart of youth" and employs such agents as pride, luxury, lust, revenge, and forgetfulness of God. His closing advice to the young man was "keep Christ, and entertain Him well. Cherish His grace; blow upon your own coal; and let Him tutor you."[19]

A young man who wrote appreciatively of the benefit Rutherford's ministry had been to his family while at Anwoth was reminded by the pastor that he was in the most dangerous part of his life, "when the lusts of youth are rank and strong." He advised the young man to acquaint himself with prayer and give diligent attention to Bible study, "that He may show you that good way that bringeth rest to the soul."[20]

Another young man Rutherford believed had made a start on the way to heaven was Robert Stuart, son of the provost of Ayr. Once again he made reference to how he had delayed somewhat before taking the gate (the way) by the end. He then urged Stuart to keep the advantage he had, to "labour for a lively sight of sin" and "make sure and fast work of conversion."[21]

John Lennox, Laird of Cally, was referred to earlier. In his first letter to him, Rutherford began by saying, "I have that confidence that your soul mindeth Christ and salvation."[22] An interest in spiritual

---

18. Rutherford to Grizzel Fullerton (letter 339), March 14, 1653, 672–73.
19. Rutherford to William Livingstone (letter 142), March 13, 1637, 271–72.
20. Rutherford to a young man in Anwoth (letter 307), n.d., 615–16.
21. Rutherford to Robert Stuart (letter 186), June 17, 1637, 363–64.
22. Rutherford to the Laird of Cally (letter 198), 1637, 388.

matters had obviously been stirred in him. But Rutherford used great freedom of speech with him "out of an earnest desire after your soul's eternal welfare." He warned him that a man cannot take his lusts to heaven with him; "such wares as these will not be welcome there."[23] In his second letter he was still exhorting him to strive to enter in at the straight gate, to lay the foundation in his youth before the devil got hold of him. He ended by saying, "If this were not so, Paul needeth not to have written to a sanctified and holy youth [a faithful preacher of the gospel], to flee the lusts of youth."[24]

One of the families Samuel Rutherford was in regular contact with was the Gordons of Airds and Earlston. William Gordon, the oldest son of Alexander Gordon of Airds and Earlston, showed in his youth a strong attachment to the Reformed faith and the Presbyterian cause. Nevertheless, Rutherford challenged him while still quite young in the following words, to which he appended something of the struggle he himself had experienced. He was ever openhearted with his young correspondents, admitting to being a man of like passions:

> Now, Sir, in your youth gather fast; your sun will mount to the meridian quickly, and thereafter decline. Be greedy of grace. Study above anything, my dear brother, to mortify your lusts. Oh, but pride of youth, vanity, lusts, idolizing of the world, and charming pleasures, take long time to root them out! As far as ye are advanced in the way to heaven, as near as ye are to Christ, as much progress as ye have made in the way of mortification, ye will find that ye are far behind, and have most of your work before you. I never took it to be so hard to be dead to my lusts and to this world.[25]

Earlston responded to the pastor's words with various questions and problems, which Rutherford sought to answer: harboring sinful thoughts, lack of assurance, sensing the withdrawal of Christ,

---

23. Rutherford to the Laird of Cally (letter 198), 1637, 389–90.

24. Rutherford to the Laird of Cally (letter 202), 1637, 397–99. A reference to 2 Timothy 2:22: "Flee also youthful lusts: but follow righteousness, faith, charity, peace, with them that call on the Lord out of a pure heart."

25. Rutherford to Earlston, Younger (letter 99), February 20, 1637, 208.

building on justification. He exhorted Earlston to give particular attention to feeding on the Word: "At our first conversion, our lord putteth the meat in young bairns' mouths with His own hand; but when we grow to some further perfection, we must take heaven by violence, and take by violence from Christ what we get." His confidence in young Earlston is clear in this same letter, when he writes, "He that can tell his tale, and send such a letter to heaven as he hath sent to Aberdeen, it is very like he will come speed with Christ."[26] William Gordon's faith did not waver in spite of the persecution he suffered in subsequent years. He was killed by a party of English dragoons after the disastrous defeat of the Covenanters at the Battle of Bothwell Bridge in 1679.[27]

---

26. Rutherford to Earlston, Younger (letter 181), June 16, 1637, 351.
27. Morton, *Galloway and the Covenanters*, 164; and Howie, *Scots Worthies*, 408.

11

Counsel to the Bereaved

One of the most moving aspects of Samuel Rutherford's pastoral work was counseling those who had lost loved ones. The early seventeenth century was a time when a variety of illnesses could often take away family members, whether through fever, typhoid, or even the plague, which was still rampant at that time. Infant deaths were especially common, for the science of midwifery was still a few centuries away.

Rutherford could sympathize readily with those who were bereaved, for he had lost not only his wife, Euphame, to a lingering, painful death after only five years of marriage but also the two children of that union, who also died very young.[1] After being a widower for ten years, he married again to Jean McMath on March 1, 1640. Two of his children by this marriage died young. Then, while he was in London at the Westminster Assembly meetings, he lost two more children. Indeed, at the time of his death in 1661, he had only one surviving child. In an appendix to Rutherford's biography, Thomas Murray lists seven children by his second wife. The surviving child, Agnes, later became Mrs. Chiesly.[2] Rutherford, therefore, had the moral right to pen the words that follow, speaking with great sympathy from personal, sad experience.

His earliest letter to one bereaved, a Christian gentlewoman on the death of a daughter, was written in 1628, barely a year after he

---

1. Murray, *Life of Samuel Rutherford*, 47–48.
2. Murray, *Life of Samuel Rutherford*, 374.

had become pastor at Anwoth.[3] This lady's daughter, a young adult, had professed faith in Christ. Rutherford's words of comfort and exhortation reveal a good level of maturity for one so inexperienced in the ministry. In counseling her, he gave first as a reason for resignation in the sad circumstances that her "long loan" (a phrase he often employed) of her daughter from the Lord had come to an end: "Indeed, that long loan of such a good daughter, an heir of grace, a member of Christ (as I believe), deserveth more thanks at your Creditor's hands, than that ye should gloom [frown] and murmur when He craveth His own!" He asked her a question he would often repeat in such correspondence: "Is she lost to you who is found to Christ?" He then cautioned her against mourning excessively: "Follow her, but envy her not; for indeed it is self-love in us maketh us mourn for them that die in the Lord." Then he counseled her not to let Satan ("the strong roaring lion") get her down, but to honor God.

Another common feature of his counseling in bereavement was to suggest that these losses served to draw the parents, or the surviving parent, closer to the Lord: "The Lord hath this way lopped your branch in taking from you many children, to the end you should grow upward, like one of the Lord's cedars, setting your heart above, where Christ is, at the right hand of the Father." He concluded his comforting letter with the attribute that she and others required at such a time, one he was indeed exercising himself just then: "Run your race with patience. Let God have His own; and ask of Him, instead of your daughter, which He hath taken from you, the daughter of faith, which is patience; and in patience possess your soul. Lift up your head: you do not know how near your redemption doth draw."[4]

Rutherford found himself often counseling his friend Viscountess Kenmure in the matter of bereavement. Early in 1629 she suffered the first of several bereavements, a daughter who died in infancy. His word of consolation to her was, as noted earlier, an approach he used on many an occasion: "Ye have not lost a child: nay she is not

3. Rutherford to a Christian gentlewoman (letter 2), April 23, 1628, 34–36.
4. Rutherford to a Christian gentlewoman (letter 2), April 23, 1628, 34–36.

lost to you who is found to Christ. She is not sent away, but only sent before, like unto a star, which going out of our sight doth not die and evanish, but shineth in another hemisphere."[5] She lost a second child in 1633.[6] The following year was one of double bereavement. She lost a third child in infancy. Rutherford believed her faith would enable her to accept this and to bow to God's sovereign purpose in it: "Acknowledge the sovereignty of God to be above the power of us mortal men, who may pluck up a flower in the bud and not be blamed for it."[7] When it was not children the viscountess lost, it was her first husband. Rutherford had lost his first wife in 1630 and could therefore write,

> I must out of some experience say, the mourning for the husband of your youth be, by God's own mouth, the heaviest worldly sorrow (Joel i, vs. 8). And though this be the weightiest burden that ever lay upon your back; yet we know (when the fields are emptied and your husband now asleep in the Lord), if ye shall wait upon Him who hideth His face for a while, and that it lieth upon God's honour and truth to fill the field, and to be a husband to the widow.... God hath dried up one channel of your love by the removal of your husband. Let now that speat [flood] run upon Christ.[8]

This latter point he would often emphasize. There was a son by her first marriage also—John, second Viscount Kenmure—who died after a few years in 1639. On this occasion Rutherford counseled her to "subscribe to the Almighty's will; put your hand to the pen, and let the cross of your Lord Jesus have your submissive and resolute AMEN." It was a Christian art to comfort oneself in the Lord, to say "I was obliged to render back again this child to the Giver."[9]

5. Rutherford to Lady Kenmure (letter 4), January 15, 1629, 41.
6. Rutherford to Lady Kenmure (letter 30), November 15, 1633, 92.
7. Rutherford to Lady Kenmure (letter 35), April 29, 1634, 97–98.
8. Rutherford to Lady Kenmure (letter 37), September 14, 1634, 100–101.
9. Rutherford to Lady Kenmure (letter 287), October 1, 1639, 565–67.

He counseled her to reverence God's will in this, pointing her to a "duration of blessedness so long as God shall live."[10]

His last communication with the viscountess concerned her brother, the Marquis of Argyll. He had been committed to the Tower of London on a charge of suspected but unproved treason. Rutherford was convinced he was a truly converted man and had evidenced this in his devotion to the cause of God and His people.[11] He did not live to hear of the beheading of the marquis at Edinburgh in May 1661.[12]

As noted earlier, one of the common uses Rutherford made of the occasion of bereavement in his counseling was seeking to draw the one bereaved into a closer walk with the Lord. For example, to a gentlewoman who had just lost her husband, who had borne a good Christian testimony, Rutherford wrote, "Know, therefore, that the wounds of your Lord Jesus are the wounds of a lover, and that he will have compassion upon a sad-hearted servant; and that Christ hath said, He will have the husband's room in your heart. He loved you in your first husband's time, and He is but wooing you still. Give Him heart and chair, house and all. He will not be made companion with any other."[13]

To another gentlewoman after the death of her husband, he similarly wrote, "In that our Lord took your husband to Himself, I know that it was that He might make room for Himself. He cutteth off your love to the creature, that ye might learn that God only is the right owner of your love."[14] Even before there was bereavement, Rutherford could give such counsel to correspondents. Lady Gaitgairth, wife of the sheriff-principal of Ayrshire, had five sons and five daughters. Though no deaths were recorded at the point of writing, he gave similar advice to her as to the bereaved: "Take no heavier lift

10. Rutherford to Lady Kenmure (letter 302), n.d., 609–10.

11. Rutherford to Lady Kenmure (letter 360), July 24, 1660, 698–99.

12. Howie, *Scots Worthies*, 256–57.

13. Rutherford to a gentlewoman (letter 105), March 7, 1637, 217.

14. Rutherford to a gentlewoman (letter 122), 1637, 246. To Lady Cardoness, similarly bereaved, he urged, "Your Lord in them is seeking you, and seek ye Him. Let none be your love and choice, and the flower of your delights, but your Lord Jesus." Letter 192, 1637, 379.

of your children than your Lord alloweth. Give them room beside your heart, but not in the yolk of your heart, where Christ should be; for then they are your idols, not your bairns. If your Lord take any of them home to His house, before the storm come on, take it well."[15]

Not all bereavements were of a family nature. When he learned that Lady Boyd, a zealous Presbyterian whom John Livingstone referred to as "a rare pattern of Christianity"[16] had lost several close friends within a short space of time, he was quick to respond. He advised her to "adore and fear the sovereignty of the great Potter, who maketh and marreth His clay-vessels when and how it pleaseth Him." Again he urged, "What love ye did bear to friends now dead, seeing they stand now in no need of it, let it fall as just legacy to Christ."[17]

Rutherford's strong belief in the sovereignty of God comes out repeatedly in his counseling of the bereaved. To one Mistress Taylor, whom he had not met but whose older son he became acquainted with while in London, he sent his commiserations on learning of the death of a younger son. This young man had been greatly blessed under the ministry of Robert Blair in St. Andrews, but the Lord had since called him home. Rutherford mentioned the two children that he himself had lost while in London, which he had accepted. He counseled Mistress Taylor to resign herself to the difficulty that she had that he had died too soon to do much for the Lord. Above all, "sovereignty must silence your thoughts.... The supreme and absolute Former of all things giveth not account of any of His matters."[18] Likewise, to Barbara Hamilton, wife of John Meine, merchant in Edinburgh, who had lost a son-in-law, he pointed to Leviticus 10:3: "And Aaron held his peace." Aaron's two sons, Nadab and Abihu, were slain because they had "offered strange fire before the LORD,

---

15. Rutherford to Lady Gaitgairth (letter 238), September 7, 1637, 473–74.

16. Livingstone, in *Memorable Characteristics*, 1:347.

17. Rutherford to Lady Boyd (letter 299), October 5, 1640, 604–6. He added, "Oh how sweet to put out many strange lovers, and to put in Christ! It is time for faith to hold fast as much of Christ as ever ye had, and to make the grip stronger, and to cleave closer to Him, seeing Christ loveth to be believed in and trusted to."

18. Rutherford to Mistress Taylor (letter 310), 1645, 620–21.

which he commanded them not" (Lev. 10:1). Aaron accepted this as from God. Therefore, wrote Rutherford to Barbara Hamilton, "Command your thoughts to be silent."[19]

While sovereignty was a major emphasis in his counseling, Rutherford also adopted other approaches—for example, the resurrection and the life to come. To a Christian friend he wrote while counseling acceptance of the loss, "But trust your faith of the resurrection of the dead in Christ to glory and immortality, will lead you to suspend your longing for her, till the morning and dawning of that day.... To believe this is best for you; and to be silent, because He hath done it, is your wisdom."[20] With another Christian friend on the death of his Christian daughter, he took another approach, arguing that we are happy if our children "outrun us in the life of grace," so then why should we be sad "if they outstrip us in the attainment of the life of glory?" He felt there was more reason to grieve if we leave children behind us "than that they are glorified and died before us."[21]

On learning of the passing of one of his regular correspondents Lady Boyd, Rutherford wrote a letter of condolence to her daughter Lady Ardross in Fife. In it he praised the way her mother had lived a life of devoted service to the Lord. She was now casting her soul's eye "upon the shining and admirably beautiful face of the Lamb." Then he lifted her thoughts to heaven, or rather brought heaven down in his comments: "Oh, what spring-time is there! Even the smelling of the odours of that great and eternally blooming Rose of Sharon for ever and ever! What a surging life is there!"[22]

In the last full year of his life, though failing in health, and only months before his own calling to come home, Rutherford continued with his pastoral counsel. One Mistress Craig had lost a son in

19. Rutherford to Barbara Hamilton (letter 311), October 15, 1645, 623–24. To David Dickson, twenty years his senior, he wrote on news of his son's death, "Ye are taught to know and adore His sovereignty, which he exerciseth over you, which is yet lustred with mercy.... He is only lopping and snedding [pruning] a fruitful tree that it may be more fruitful.... Go on, and faint not." Letter 298, May 28, 1640, 602–3.

20. Rutherford to a Christian friend (letter 315), 1645, 629–30.

21. Rutherford to a Christian brother (letter 316), February 24, 1646, 630–31.

22. Rutherford to Lady Ardross (letter 321), February 24, 1646, 639–40.

tragic circumstances, a drowning accident in France. He counseled the bereaved mother with a letter that gave nine different reasons why she should be perfectly resigned to his departure. The sting was taken out because the young man had given good proof of spiritual life in him, and he was now perfected and glorified. Above all, she should accept that the time of his departure had been determined from eternity. Therefore godly submission should quiet her mind and silence her heart. "It is," he wrote, "the art and skill of faith to appreciate what God has done here"; therefore she should not faint under this visitation or despise it.[23]

23. Rutherford to Mistress Craig (letter 361), August 4, 1660, 699–701.

12

Counseling the Dying

As well as giving counsel to young and old, whatever their standing in society, Samuel Rutherford took time to write to some of his long-standing friends who were about to depart this life, holding before them the sure prospect of the joys of heaven. He continued to do this even when his own health was deteriorating.

George Gillespie (1613–1648)

Samuel Rutherford had known George Gillespie from his earliest days at Anwoth, when the latter was appointed chaplain to the Kenmure family. Alexander Whyte describes how these two brethren developed an intimate friendship, being of like mind in so many spiritual matters of the day, often spending time in prayer together:

> One day, rising off their knees in the woods of Kenmure Castle, the two men took one another by the hand and swore a covenant that all their days, and amid all the trials they saw were coming to Scotland and her Church, they would remain fast friends, would often think of one another, would often name one another before God in prayer, and would regularly write to one another, and that not on church questions only and on the books they were reading, but more especially on the life of God in their own souls.[1]

Unfortunately, there are only three letters remaining of all that correspondence. In the first of these, Rutherford unburdened him-

1. Whyte, *Samuel Rutherford and Some of His Correspondents*, 152.

self to his young friend, thirteen years his junior, of the difficulty he had in adjusting to his new surroundings in Aberdeen: "Brother, remember our old covenant, and pray for me, and write to me your case."[2] Six months later he wrote of his conviction that the cause of Christ would triumph in Scotland.[3]

Gillespie was ordained minister at Wemyss in Fife in April 1638, moving to the High Kirk of Edinburgh in 1642. Rutherford and Gillespie were together as Scottish commissioners to the Westminster Assembly from 1643 to 1647. The thirty-year-old Gillespie was the most active of the Scots in the debates, making 167 speeches, surpassing Rutherford with his 148 and Henderson with 83.[4] Of his contribution their fellow commissioner Robert Baillie wrote, "None in all the Assembly did reason more, nor more pertinently, than Mr Gillespie: he is an excellent youth; my heart blesses God in his behalf."[5]

Gillespie contracted tuberculosis soon after his return from London. Hearing of his illness, Rutherford wrote to him, commending him for his life's work, short though it was: "Christ in and by you hath done more than twenty, yea, an hundred grey-haired and godly pastors." His doing was over; believing in Christ's work was now his last act: "All your wants, dear brother, be upon Him: ye are His debtors; grace must sum and subscribe your accounts as paid."[6]

Rutherford visited his old friend Gillespie the day before he died, saying, "The day, I hope, is dawning and breaking in your soul, that shall never have an end." Gillespie replied, "It is not broken yet, but though I walk in darkness and see no light, I will trust in the name of the Lord and stay upon my God." Rutherford then asked him, "Doth not your soul love Christ above all things? He replied, I love him heartily: who ever knew anything of Him but would love Him?"[7]

---

2. Rutherford to George Gillespie (letter 144), March 13, 1637, 274–75.

3. Rutherford to George Gillespie (letter 253), September 9, 1637, 497.

4. John Keddie, "George Gillespie and the Westminster Assembly," *Scottish Reformation Society Historical Journal* 8 (2018): 50.

5. Howie, *Scots Worthies*, 194.

6. Rutherford to George Gillespie (letter 324), September 27, 1648, 644.

7. Keddie, "George Gillespie and the Westminster Assembly," 56.

Rutherford did not forget Gillespie's widow, Margaret. Having written at the end of his letter to the dying man, "Ye must leave the wife to a more choice husband, and the children to a better Father," he wrote to the widow, who, months after the passing of her husband, was grieving the additional loss of a son, Archibald. The Lord saw that she was able, by His grace, to bear the loss of both husband and child. As in earlier cases, Rutherford counseled her complete acceptance of the circumstances: "I should wish that, at the reading of this, ye may fall down and make a surrender of those that are gone, and of those that are yet alive, to Him. And for you, let Him have all; and wait for Himself, for He will come, and will not tarry. Live by faith, and the peace of God guard your heart."[8]

James Durham (1622–1658)

After studying divinity at Glasgow under David Dickson,[9] James Durham became for a time chaplain to the king's family, "in which station, though the times were most difficult, as abounding with snares and temptations, he did so wisely and faithfully acquit himself, that there was conviction left upon the consciences of all who observed him."[10] Thereafter he served in two charges in Glasgow. Robert Baillie praised him as "one of the most gracious, wise and able preachers in this isle."[11] When the unhappy division of the Covenanters into Resolutioners and Protesters occurred, Durham would not take sides. Howie describes how "his healing disposition, and great moderation of spirit, remarkably appeared when this Church was grievously divided betwixt the Resolutioners and Protesters; he would never give his judgment on either side, and used to say, that 'division was worse by far than either.' He was equally respected by

8. Rutherford to Mistress Gillespie (letter 326), August 14, 1649, 647.

9. He had begun study at the University of St. Andrews but left without obtaining a degree "to pursue the life of a country gentleman." David Lachman, introduction to Durham, *Dying Man's Testament*, iii.

10. Howie, *Scots Worthies*, 223–24.

11. As quoted in the introduction to letter 351, 685.

both parties."[12] As noted in chapter 1, his work *Concerning Scandal* came too late to effect any change.

Rutherford wrote to him a few days before his death, the only extant letter, reminding him of how he had preached to others of the way to heaven and "the glory of the home beyond death." Now when He says, "'Come and see,' it will be your gain to obey, and go out and meet the Bridegroom." Rutherford assured him that he should not concern himself about his family, for God had said, "Leave them to Me, and come up hither." His own health declining by this time, Rutherford closed his brief letter by holding the prospect of heaven before him: "It is an unknown land to you, who were never there before; but the land is good, and the company before the throne desirable, and He who sitteth on the throne is His lone a sufficient heaven."[13]

James Guthrie (1614–1661)

James Guthrie's first contact with Samuel Rutherford was when the latter became professor of divinity at the New College, St. Andrews. Both James and his cousin William Guthrie benefited greatly from the lectures, debates, and weekly gatherings for conference and prayer. James became minister first at Lauder, then at Stirling. As he signed the National Covenant with some initial hesitation, he remarked to those around him, "I know that I shall die for what I have done this day, but I cannot die in a better cause."[14]

Three letters from Rutherford to Guthrie, a fellow Protester, are extant. From London Rutherford wrote in what was undoubtedly a downcast mood, saying that he coveted being in the hearts and prayers of the saints, and he spoke of himself being at low ebb: "Yea, as low as any soul can be, and do scarcely know where I am."[15]

---

12. Howie, *Scots Worthies*, 226.

13. Rutherford to James Durham (letter 351), June 15, 1658, 685.

14. Whyte, *Samuel Rutherford and Some of His Correspondents*, 132. The remark may in part be occasioned by his path being crossed by the city executioner as he turned in at the gate of the Greyfriars church. In a day of omens, this made him hesitate, yet he went ahead and signed. Smellie, *Men of the Covenant*, 89.

15. Rutherford to James Guthrie (letter 319), January 30, 1646, 637.

Fourteen years later he addressed a letter to Guthrie and eleven other men who had been arrested in the process of composing a letter of congratulation to Charles II, pledging their allegiance but also reminding the king of his obligation to the covenant that he and the nation had signed. Rutherford was persuaded that it was for the cause of Christ they were suffering. About himself he wrote, "If Christ doth own me, let me be in the grave in a bloody winding-sheet, and go from the scaffold in four quarters, to grave or no grave. I am his debtor, to seal with sufferings this precious truth."[16] This was not to be the way his life would end.

To James Guthrie, in prison and about to become the protomartyr of the Second Reformation, he wrote in prophetic strain, "Happy are ye if you give testimony of your preferring Jesus Christ to all powers. And the Lord will make the innocency and Christian loyalty of his defamed and despised witnesses in this land to shine to after-generations." He counseled Guthrie not to fear, forgive his enemies, as Rutherford would do (see the conclusion), and to cast the burden of his family on the Lord. He concluded by saying, "Your blood is precious in His sight. The everlasting consolations of the Lord bear you up and give you hope; for your salvation (if not deliverance) is concluded."[17]

Guthrie certainly was borne up in his last days. He told his wife that he was actually more blessed than the Marquis of Argyll, "for my lord was beheaded, but I am to be hanged on a tree as my Saviour was."[18] Among his last words were these: "Jesus Christ is my light and life, my righteousness, my strength, and my salvation, and all my desire. Him! O Him! I do, with all the strength of my soul, commend to you. Bless Him O my soul, from henceforth, even for ever!"[19] The short man who could not bow, as Cromwell called him, was hanged

16. Rutherford to James Guthrie and other imprisoned brethren in Edinburgh (letter 357), 1660, 693.

17. Rutherford to James Guthrie (letter 362), February 15, 1661, 701–2.

18. Smellie, *Men of the Covenant*, 97.

19. Howie, *Scots Worthies*, 266.

at the cross of Edinburgh on June 1, 1661. Rutherford was already home with the Lord.

Conversations with the Dying Viscount Kenmure

Returning from a visit to David Dickson in Irvine, Rutherford called at Kenmure Castle, twenty miles from Anwoth, only to learn of the quickly deteriorating health of the viscount. He acceded to the request to remain with him in his terminal illness. Marion McNaught was in attendance throughout those difficult days, from August 31 through September 12, 1634. The family chaplain, George Gillespie, was also present.

In his youth Kenmure had made a clear profession of faith. This may have been when he spent time in the household of Rev. John Welsh (or Welch) when the latter was in exile in France at Saint-Jean-d'Angély. When he came back to Rusco Castle in Anwoth, one sign of spiritual life could be seen in the way he got Anwoth separated from Kirkmabreck and Kirkdale to become a parish with its own minister.[20]

Gordon's marriage to Lady Jane Campbell took place in 1628. A year later they moved to Edinburgh. There, it would seem, his mind was turned away from spiritual matters and a pilgrim life to a more worldly minded outlook. He had been created Viscount of Kenmure and Lord of Lochinvar by Charles I, who was seeking to ingratiate himself with the nobility. Kenmure hoped for further advancement.[21] Rutherford noted the change in the viscount, the lack of interest in spiritual affairs. This led to some attempts to get the viscountess to point her husband once again to renewed spiritual interests:

> Madam, stir up your husband to lay hold upon the covenant, and to do good. What hath he to do with the world? It is not his inheritance. Desire him to make home-over [homeward], and

20. Samuel Rutherford, *Conversations with a Dying Man* (Stornoway, Scotland: Reformation Press, 2017), 10. Originally published in 1649 with the title *The Last and Heavenly Speeches, and Glorious Departure of John Gordon Viscount Kenmure.*

21. Rutherford, *Conversations with a Dying Man*, 11–12.

> put to his hand to lay one stone or two upon the wall of God's house before he go hence.[22]

> Madam, it is part of the truth of your profession to drop words in the ear of your noble husband continually of eternity, judgment, death, hell, heaven, the honourable profession, the sins of his father's house.[23]

The reason for Rutherford going into print with *Conversations with a Dying Man* is found in the dedication—"For the Whole Nobility of Scotland, and others having a voice in Parliament or Committees"—which was also in keeping with what the dying viscount wished. The key to the work is in the following phrase: "The heavy pangs of conscience and torment of mind, wherein a nobleman, not long since, was exercised upon his deathbed for not countenancing the cause of God when he was publicly called thereto in Parliament."[24]

Kenmure had attended Parliament but feigned ill health, excusing himself from attending rather than take a stand at a key time in the nation's struggles for the purity of the church. "Therefore," wrote Rutherford, "it pleased the Lord to afflict his body with sickness, to shake his soul with fears, to drop in bitterness in his spirit, and make him altogether sensible of the power of eternal wrath for his own good and the good of others in after ages."[25] "Remember therefore," the pastor also wrote in his dedication, "that conscience is placed in the soul as God's deputy and notary."[26]

Seven conversations took place between the pastor and the viscount. In the first, Kenmure confessed to not having settled his accounts with God. Howie records how in his youth Kenmure had been "somewhat irreligious and profane, which, when he arrived at manhood, broke out into more gross acts of wickedness.... The most part of his life, after he advanced in years, he spent like the rich man

---

22. Rutherford to Lady Kenmure (letter 28), April 1, 1633, 88.
23. Rutherford to Lady Kenmure (letter 30), November 15, 1633, 91.
24. Rutherford, *Conversations with a Dying Man*, 20.
25. Rutherford, *Conversations with a Dying Man*, 20–24.
26. Rutherford, *Conversations with a Dying Man*, 24.

in the Gospel, casting down barns, and building greater ones; for at his houses of Rusco and Kenmuir [*sic*] he was much employed in building, parking, planting, and seeking worldly honours."[27] Admitting to this, Kenmure urged his pastor, "Therefore stay with me and show me the marks of a child of God."[28]

In the second conversation, Rutherford urged on Kenmure the need for conviction of sin and deep humiliation. There was need for him to be "weary and laden," for Christ's commission from the Father was only to the "broken-hearted, captives, prisoners, mourners in Zion" (see Isa. 61:1–3). At this point Rutherford concluded the session with prayer once again.[29]

The third conversation found Kenmure deeply moved and in anguish over all his years of unrepented sin. "Then he covered his face with a linen cloth, and burst into tears and wept sore." He eventually "prayed divinely and graciously, with tears."[30]

In their fourth conversation together, it was clear that Kenmure was resorting more to prayer. He had also charged his pastor to go to his closet and engage in prayer in his behalf; other godly friends were likewise asked to pray. Two were sent to Kenmure Wood for that purpose. At the end of this time together, it appeared the viscount was closer to having made his peace with God.

But in the fifth conversation, the viscount admitted to unconfessed sin, in particular his desertion of the last Parliament. This was the most difficult part of the whole interlude. For at this point Rutherford read several Scripture passages, including Hebrews 6:1–8, which describes reprobates, leading Kenmure to despair. The pastor, however, continued to press him till he professed faith in the language of Job 13:15—"Though he slay me, yet will I trust in him." The pastor's response to this was, "Your loving and longing for Christ is a fire of God's kindling. My Lord, persuade yourself, you are graven

27. Howie, *Scots Worthies*, 154. Howie's chapter at this point contains the whole account of the 1649 edition of the conversations.

28. Rutherford, *Conversations with a Dying Man*, 33.

29. Rutherford, *Conversations with a Dying Man*, 35–36.

30. Rutherford, *Conversations with a Dying Man*, 37–38.

on the palms of God's hands." After this Kenmure was much in the exercise of prayer.[31]

At their sixth meeting, Kenmure seemed to have the assurance of his salvation, believing that Christ was in his heart.[32] At their last conversation, Kenmure was strongly asserting that he would not let go of the grip he had of Christ, adding once again, "Though He slay me, yet will I trust Him." He passed away peacefully as his pastor was praying for him.[33]

A few weeks afterward, writing to the widowed viscountess, Rutherford said, "In this late visitation that hath befallen your Ladyship, ye have seen God's love and care, in such a measure that I thought our lord brake the sharp point of the cross, and made us and your Ladyship see Christ take possession and infeftment [possession of inheritable property] upon earth, of him who is now reigning and triumphing with the hundred and forty and four thousand who stand with the Lamb on Mount Zion."[34]

Rutherford had two main reasons for publishing *Conversations with a Dying Man* in 1649. It would serve to remind the nobles and gentry of Scotland of their duty to the kirk. It also served to show the reality of conversion in the life of Viscount Kenmure, the fruit of repentance to life being eminently displayed in this dying man. The fruit of his conversion can also be seen in the thoroughness of his dying testimony.

The viscount testified to all kinds of people—his household, relatives, friends who came to visit, and ministers—expressing to them all his own mistaken life and his newfound faith in Christ. To his sister, who was a Roman Catholic, he urged the forsaking of Rome, expressing at the same time his own assurance of salvation and his firm belief that he was going to be with Christ.[35] He exhorted many

---

31. Rutherford, *Conversations with a Dying Man*, 41–47.
32. Rutherford, *Conversations with a Dying Man*, 51–53.
33. Rutherford, *Conversations with a Dying Man*, 74–76.
34. Rutherford to Lady Kenmure (letter 39), November 29, 1634, 104.
35. Rutherford, *Conversations with a Dying Man*, 58, 71.

who came to him on his deathbed to seek the Lord while He might be found, as he himself had just done.[36]

Another great concern of his was the snares of youth. To two young men he said,

> Suffer not, therefore, this example that you see of me to slip unobserved, but make your best use of it. I entreat you to give your youth to Jesus Christ, for it is the most precious offer and acceptable gift you can give Him. Give not your youth to the devil and your lusts, and then reserve nothing to Jesus Christ but your old rotten bones. It is to be feared that then he will not accept you. Learn therefore to watch and take example of me.[37]

He spoke to some of the clergy. For example, he admonished James Irving of Parton to be more painstaking in his work and shepherd his flock with greater care.[38] He regretted to George Gillespie that he had not heeded his pastoral advice as he should have done.[39] A long conversation took place with Bishop Andrew Lamb of Galloway, in which the viscount urged him not to enforce the Five Articles of Perth on the congregations within his bounds, as these were not "things indifferent."[40] He also spoke to all his servants and asked that the poor of the parish be not neglected.[41]

Howie summed up the account of the viscount's last days for those who might object to his being remembered alongside other worthies:

> What did the most eminent saint that ever was in Scotland, or anywhere else, until enabled by the grace of God? So it was with reference to him; for no sooner was he made partaker of this, than he gave a most ample and faithful testimony for his truths and interest; and although the Lord did not see it proper

36. Rutherford, *Conversations with a Dying Man*, 57, 58, 62, 66–67.
37. Rutherford, *Conversations with a Dying Man*, 59–60, 63.
38. Rutherford, *Conversations with a Dying Man*, 60–61.
39. Rutherford, *Conversations with a Dying Man*, 61–62.
40. Rutherford, *Conversations with a Dying Man*, 64–65.
41. Rutherford, *Conversations with a Dying Man*, 68–69, 72.

that he should serve Him after this manner in his day and generation, yet He, no doubt, accepted of the will for the deed; and why should we not enrol his name among these Worthies on earth, seeing He hath written his name among the living in Jerusalem.[42]

42. Howie, *Scots Worthies*, 170.

Conclusion

Samuel Rutherford's life was set in troublesome times for the church in Scotland. In the early years of his ministry at Anwoth, he could see the clouds gathering. In a letter to Marion McNaught, a year and a half before his exile to Aberdeen, he noted, "There is a cloud gathering and a storm coming. This land shall be turned upside down."[1] At the same time, however, he was confident that Zion would be built up again. In a sermon titled "The Deliverance of the Kirk of God," from Jeremiah 50:4–5, he said, "The Kirk of God never sooner enters in any trouble, but they have the Lord's backhand [bond] given unto them that they shall be brought out of it again; and they have law burrows [legal security] and caution of the Lord that death, hell, and all sort of troubles shall not do at them [take effect on them] to destroy them."[2]

To Lady Culross he wrote, "This poor persecuted kirk, this lily among the thorns, shall blossom, and laugh upon the gardener; the husbandman's blessings shall light upon it."[3] "However it be," he wrote to Alexander Gordon of Earlston, "I avouch it before the world, that the tabernacle of the Lord shall again be in the midst of Scotland, and the glory of the Lord shall dwell in beauty, as the light of many days in one, in this land."[4]

---

1. Rutherford to Marion McNaught (letter 50), April 22, 1635, 121–22.

2. Rutherford, *Quaint Sermons*, 154.

3. Rutherford to Lady Culross (letter 74), December 30, 1636, 157.

4. Rutherford to Alexander Gordon of Earlston (letter 201), 1637, 395. To Lord Craighall he wrote, "Howbeit this day be not Christ's, the morrow shall be His. I believe

Rutherford lived to witness the triumph of the Covenanters and the years of triumph for the Presbyterian cause known as the Second Reformation. He lived also to see the unity of a church divided into Resolutioners and Protesters, as outlined previously in chapter 1. A further reason for disunity lay in the failure of the Covenanters to gain the support of a good number of men of position and title, though Rutherford had tried to secure the backing of many. Smellie explains, "The larger proportion of their adherents had come from the middle class and from the peasantry. Many of the nobles were hostile. Earls and barons and knights, with lives which were only too ungoverned and rough, and private sins that they wished to keep undisturbed, resented the faithfulness of the Church's rebukes and the supervision she tried to exercise over their households and manners. They paid lip-service till the king came back."[5] Added to this, the poverty of some of the ruling families led them to side with the king, and not the church, in the expectation of revenue from forfeited estates.[6]

Rutherford did not live to see the church restored, for even as he lay dying, the "Drunken Parliament"[7] was in process of dismantling all that had been accomplished since 1638. After six and a half months, having met from New Year's Day 1661 to July 12, 393 acts were passed, strengthening the power and authority of Charles II over the nation and the church. For example, the general Recissory Act of March 28, 1661, annulled the work of all parliaments from 1640 to 1648.[8]

Preaching had been the breath of life to Samuel Rutherford. Being deprived of this for a time, as noted previously, was what hurt him most while in Aberdeen. With the exception of his time there, he

---

assuredly that our Lord will repair the old waste places and His ruined houses in Scotland; and that this wilderness shall yet blossom as the rose." Letter 227, August 10, 1637, 449.

5. Smellie, *Men of the Covenant*, 51.

6. Smellie, *Men of the Covenant*, 52.

7. So called because often "it was when they were stupefied by their carousels that the senators determined on their revolutionary enactments." Smellie, *Men of the Covenant*, 59.

8. Donaldson, *Scotland: James V to James VII*, 359, 362; Burleigh, *Church History of Scotland*, 236–38; and Smellie, *Men of the Covenant*, 56–59.

preached in Anwoth, St. Andrews, and during the years in London until his health gave way. He loved to extol free grace:

> But I owe as many praises and thanks to free grace as would lie betwixt me and the utmost border of the highest heaven, suppose ten thousand heavens were all laid above other.... All our stability, and the strength of our salvation is anchored and fastened upon free grace.[9]

> Now I will bless the Lord that ever there was such a thing as the free grace of God, and a free ransom given for sold souls.[10]

Another theme he brought before his correspondents was the second coming of Christ, a prominent doctrine in the New Testament. He had at least two reasons for this. First, it was to encourage them in difficult circumstances and to live in the expectation of His soon coming again. For Rutherford, in particular, the great attraction was that he would meet and be united to the Bridegroom:

> But yet a little while and our Lord will come again. Scotland's sky will clear again, her moment must go over.[11]

> O for the coming of the Bridegroom! Oh, when shall I see the Bridegroom and the Bride meet in the clouds, and kiss each other! Oh, when will we get our day, and our heart's fill of that love! It is not for nothing that it is said, "Christ in you the hope of glory!" (Col. i, 27).[12]

---

9. Rutherford to John Kennedy (letter 85), January 6, 1637, 180. To William Rigge of Athernie, he wrote, "Oh, but we have cause to carry low sails, and to cleave fast to free grace, free, free grace! Blessed be our Lord that ever that way was found out. If my one foot were in heaven and my soul half in, if free-will and corruption were absolutely lords of me, I should never win wholly in. Oh, but the sweet, new, and living way, that Christ hath struck up to our home, is a safe way!" Letter 273, September 30, 1637, 529.

10. Rutherford to Alexander Gordon of Garloch (letter 217), 1637, 426. See also Rutherford to the following: Fulwood, the Younger (letter 224), July 10, 1637, 436–37; Robert Blair (letter 254), September 9, 1637, 498–99; Lady Boyd (letter 277), 1637, 536–38; and Earlston the Elder (letter 323), May 15, 1646, 643.

11. Rutherford to Marion McNaught (letter 51), 1635, 123.

12. Rutherford to John Kennedy (letter 130), n.d., 255–56.

> Our Master will rend the clouds, and will be upon us quickly, and clear our cause, and bring us all out in blacks and whites. O day, dawn! O time, run fast! O Bridegroom, post, post, fast, that we may meet. O heavens, cleave in two, that that bright face and head may set itself through the clouds![13]

Rutherford's production of thirteen major theological treatises, which amounted to more than seven thousand pages, not to mention several shorter works, in addition to his teaching commitment and preaching and pastoral work are nothing short of phenomenal. It may help to account for his health giving way.

It may also explain why he did not produce a biblical commentary. The seventeenth century saw the publication in Scotland of several outstanding expositions of Scripture, several of which have been reprinted in recent times. In Scotland the lead was taken by Rutherford's friend David Dickson, minister of the gospel at Irvine, with his commentary on Hebrews. There followed other fine works by men such as George Hutcheson, minister at the Tolbooth, Edinburgh; James Ferguson, minister at Kilwinning; Alexander Nisbet, who succeeded Dickson at Irvine; and James Durham, minister in Glasgow.[14] In one of Rutherford's letters to Dickson, he made reference to Dickson's work on Hebrews as being "in great request with

---

13. Rutherford to Fulwood, the Younger (letter 224), July 10, 1637, 437. See also Rutherford to the following: Lady Kenmure (letter 4), January 15, 1629, 41–42; Lady Kenmure (letter 5), September 14, 1629, 43–44; Marion McNaught (letter 16), n.d., 62–64; and letter 17, n.d., 65; Lady Kenmure (letter 21), January 14, 1632, 72–74; Marion McNaught (letter 26), September 19, 1632, 83–85; and letter 34, April 25, 1634, 96–97; Lady Kenmure (letter 56), January 18, 1636, 129–31; and letter 95, 1637, 200–201; Robert Glendinning (letter 136), March 13, 1637, 264–65; and Thomas Garven (letter 152), March 14, 1637, 283–84.

14. George Christie, "Scripture Exposition in Scotland in the Seventeenth Century," *Records of the Scottish Church History Society* 1, part 3 (1926): 97, 111. Works by Dickson on Hebrews (1635), the New Testament Epistles (1659), Matthew (1647), and Psalms (1653–54); works by Hutcheson on the twelve Minor Prophets (1655), John (1657), and Job (1669); works by Ferguson on Philippians and Colossians (1656), Galatians and Ephesians (1659), and Thessalonians (1675); works by Nisbet on 1 and 2 Peter (1658) and Ecclesiastes (1694); works by Durham on Revelation (1658), Song of Solomon (1668), and Job (1759).

all who would be acquainted with Christ's Testament." He added, "I purpose, God willing, to set about Hosea, and to try if I can get it to the press here."[15] If this was intended to be part of the commentaries that Dickson was perhaps editing, it never materialized. Hutcheson appears to have done that volume instead. Another work on Isaiah seems to have been begun but has not survived.[16]

In an age of faction and controversy like many others, the word *toleration* was not at the forefront of Rutherford's vocabulary. He did not have the irenic spirit of one such as James Durham. Nor could he ever fit the description given of the character of James Guthrie:

> His temper was very steady and composed; he could reason upon the most subtle points with great solidity, and, when every one else was warm, his temper was never ruffled. At any time when indecent heats or wranglings happened to occur when reasoning, it was his ordinary custom to say, "enough of this; let us go to some other subject; we are warm, and can dispute no longer with advantage." Perhaps he had the greatest mixture of fervent zeal and sweet calmness in his temper, of any man in his time.[17]

By contrast, Rutherford showed toward the Resolutioners on many occasions "an acrimoniousness which was far from admirable."[18] If he showed an acrimoniousness in debate and a lack of toleration of Arminian and episcopal opponents, he nevertheless showed his deep concern for the Presbyterian church in Scotland by accepting, if with reluctance, his removal from Anwoth to St. Andrews and by his turning down appointments in universities in Europe. He was neither a career preacher nor concerned to carve out an academic reputation for himself.

Much has been made of the way in which Taylor Innes, in his excellent sketch of Rutherford's life, highlighted a phrase in one of

---

15. Rutherford to David Dickson (letter 110), March 7, 1637, 226.
16. Rutherford to David Dickson (letter 110), March 7, 1637, 226n1.
17. Howie, *Scots Worthies*, 257–58.
18. Smellie, *Men of the Covenant*, 70.

Rutherford's letters to David Dickson: "I am made of extremes."[19] Many have followed this—for example, Alexander Whyte in his work *Samuel Rutherford and Some of His Correspondents*—devoting a chapter to this theme.[20] Rather than dissect the man's character on the basis of this one phrase, as some have done, this author would prefer rather to point, more constructively, to a quotation from Scripture that he applied in preaching to himself and to his hearers and also twice in his correspondence.[21]

When preaching from Luke 15:29–32 on the forlorn son around 1640, Rutherford said that the ground of the anger of the elder brother ("he was angry, and would not go in") was because the younger son had come home to Christ: "And what is the ground of the hatred that is between the followers of Christ and the rest of the world?" He referred them to John 15:19,[22] paraphrasing it in these words: "You shall get the world's malice and all the quarrel that the world shall have against you shall be only because you are my disciples." Referring then to his Scottish context, he said, "There cannot be a kindly peace between Prelatists and Papists, and those who have bound themselves in a covenant with God." Opposition, then, was to be expected from "the men of the world."[23]

It was in this context that he quoted Jeremiah 15:10: "Woe is me, my mother, that thou hast borne me a man of strife and a man of contention to the whole earth." On this verse in Jeremiah John Calvin commented, "He calls himself a man of strife, not only because he was constrained to contend with the people, for this he had in common with all the prophets. God does not send them to flatter or to please the world; they must therefore contend with the world. Jeremiah's very presence among his people ensured contention and

19. Rutherford to David Dickson (letter 168), May 1, 1637, 315.

20. Whyte, *Samuel Rutherford and Some of His Correspondents*, 10–18.

21. Rutherford to John Kennedy (letter 75), January 1, 1637, 160; and Rutherford to Marion McNaught (letter 80), January 3, 1637, 169.

22. "If ye were of the world, the world would love his own: but because ye are not of the world, but I have chosen you out of the world, therefore the world hateth you."

23. Rutherford, *Quaint Sermons*, 319.

strife."[24] Rutherford's comment on the verse was, "And the reason of all their envy is because the Word of God is his delight."[25]

Rutherford, like the prophet, was captive to the Word. For him there were no nonfundamentals.[26] Nor were there what some were beginning to call "things indifferent."[27] If he is to be characterized by any phrase, surely it is fitting that he be seen as one, alongside many others in the ministry and in the land, who felt compelled to contend for the truth of God's Word, for the doctrines of grace, and for the crown rights of the Redeemer, whether or not this contending engendered strife.

Rutherford's whole personal spiritual life had been one of seeking to know Christ and to be more and more like Him. In his last days he was heard to remark, "'Tis no easy thing to be a Christian, but for me, I have gotten the victory, and Christ is holding out both arms to embrace me.... I betake me to Christ for sanctification, as well as justification.... He is made of God to me wisdom, righteousness, sanctification, and redemption."[28] Thus sanctification had been

---

24. John Calvin, *Commentary on the Book of Jeremiah and the Lamentations* (Grand Rapids: Baker, 1981), 1:268.

25. Rutherford, *Quaint Sermons*, 319.

26. In a letter to Patrick Gillespie in 1651 he stated,

> School-heads talk of fundamentals and non-fundamentals; and, say they, "The present controversy is not about fundamentals: ministers may keep their places, peace, and stipends, and make less din." But are non-fundamentals nothing? I would choose rather not be brought up at school, than to grow so subtile and wily by school distinctions, [as] to decline the cross. Sir, you divide not from others for nothing; you contend not for nothing; you suffer not for nothing. They that will be unfaithful in little will be unfaithful in much.... That Christ ought to be a King in Scotland, and the people ought to employ the liberty that Christ hath bought to them with His blood, is among fundamentals with me.

Letter 337, n.d., 669–70.

27. In a sermon on Isaiah 49:1–4, he said, "And ken ye what some men have devised? They have devised what they are pleased to call *indifferent* things, indifferent truths in religion; and think that they may sell twenty stone weight of them, and have enough behind." Rutherford, *Fourteen Communion Sermons*, 143.

28. "Some of the Last Words of Mr. Rutherford," in *Joshua Redivivus*, ed. Robert McWard, 522–23. The full text of his last days is also contained in Howie, *Scots Worthies*, 237–40.

with him a preoccupation of a lifetime. As Marcus Loane has pointed out, "The supreme value of his ministry was due to the pains he took with the spiritual development of his own soul."[29]

Many have ended their accounts of Rutherford's life by highlighting some of his last words, such as the following: "Let my Lord's name be exalted; and, if He will, let my name be grinded to pieces, that He may be all in all. If He should slay me ten thousand times, I will trust. Mine eyes shall see my Redeemer: these very eyes of mine, and none other for me."[30]

His friend and colleague in the ministry Robert Blair was present with him toward the end. Blair asked him, "What think ye now of Christ?"

He replied, "I shall live and adore Him. Glory! glory to my Creator and my Redeemer for ever! Glory shines in Immanuel's land. Oh! for arms to embrace Him! Oh! for a well-tuned harp!"[31]

Rutherford never experienced anything like the blessing that David Dickson saw at Irvine nor the outpouring at Kirk of Shotts under the preaching of the young John Livingstone. Nevertheless, preaching and pastoral care remained his first love. Consider, in closing, therefore, the pastoral spirit of the dying man in his words to those who visited him in his last days. On March 17, three gentlewomen came to see him. He exhorted them to read the Scriptures, to devote themselves to prayer, and to be much in communion with God. At the same time he expressed his forgiveness to the brethren in the presbytery and in the New College, feeling that he had been marginalized by them because of his strong Protester stance.[32]

That same day four brethren came to see him. His words to them were, "Dear brethren, do all for Him: pray for Christ, preach for Christ, feed the flock committed to your charge for Christ, do

---

29. Marcus L. Loane, *Makers of Religious Freedom: Henderson, Rutherford, Bunyan, Baxter* (London: Inter-Varsity, 1960), 93.

30. "Some of the Last Words of Mr. Rutherford," 525.

31. "Some of the Last Words of Mr. Rutherford," 525.

32. "Some of the Last Words of Mr. Rutherford," 525.

all for Christ."[33] He cautioned them against what was too prevalent in those days—an attitude of men pleasing. He expressed a desire that the youth in the New College where he had labored for so many years might be "fed with sound knowledge." He even made so bold as to send a commission to the St. Andrews presbytery "to appear, for God and His cause, and adhere to the doctrine of the covenant, and have a care of the flock committed to their charge.... Let them feed the flock out of love, preach for God, visit and catechise for God, and do all for God." As Mr. Vilant, one of the four brethren, closed their meeting in prayer at his request, his parting words were a charge once more to feed the flock out of love.[34]

It was a deep regret to Rutherford that he would not obtain a martyr's death and crown. In the words of the last stanza of Mrs. Cousins's paraphrase of his last words:

> They've summoned me before them,
> But there I may not come,
> My Lord says, "Come up hither,"
> My Lord says, "Welcome home!"
> My kingly King, at His white throne,
> My presence doth command,
> Where glory—glory dwelleth
> In Immanuel's land.[35]

Having given his last pastoral counsel, he departed this life at five in the morning on March 29 as he had predicted, "sleeping in the bosom of the Almighty."[36]

---

33. "Some of the Last Words of Mr. Rutherford," 526.

34. "Some of the Last Words of Mr. Rutherford," 527.

35. Bonar, appendix to *Letters of Samuel Rutherford*, 744.

36. Rutherford to a Christian gentlewoman (letter 2), April 23, 1628, 34. Words used to counsel a gentlewoman who had lost her adult Christian daughter: "Do you think her lost, when she is but sleeping in the bosom of the Almighty?"

Appendix 1

The Source of Early Protestant Teachings in Aberdeen

Certain patterns of trade between Aberdeen and the Continent are discernible, dating back in some cases before the fifteenth century. The burgh had close contacts with the Low Countries in the sixteenth century, especially at the time of the Reformation.[1] A link had been formed between Aberdeen and Campvere, where some Aberdonians had settled. Several of them, members of burgess families such as the Skenes, Gordons, Gregorys, Lumsdens, and Allardyces, held from time to time or successively the position of Conservator of Scottish Privileges there.[2] There were also trading, cultural, and diplomatic contacts with Denmark.[3] The port most closely associated with Aberdeen was Danzig.[4] During the 1520s both northern

1. Stuart, *Extracts from the Council Register*, 1:18; V. E. Clark, *The Port of Aberdeen* (Aberdeen: D. Wylie and Son, 1921), 6, 7; Robert Anderson, "The Aberdonian Abroad," part 1, *Aberdeen University Review* 9 (1921–1922): 41; J. A. Fleming, *Flemish Influence in Britain* (Glasgow: Jackson, Wylie, 1930), 1:335; and William Kennedy, *Annals of Aberdeen* (London, 1818), 2:11–12.

2. Anderson, "Aberdonian Abroad," part 1, 41; and Clark, *Port of Aberdeen*, 19.

3. Stuart, *Extracts from the Council Register*, 1:333; Thomas Thomson, ed., *Acts of the Parliaments of Scotland* (London, 1814), 2:302; Hugh Ferrie, "Some Pre-Reformation Scots in Denmark," *Innes Review* 3 (1952): 130–31; and Anderson, "Aberdonian Abroad," part 1, 44.

4. J. H. Burton, ed., *Register of the Privy Council of Scotland* (Edinburgh, 1877), 1:191, 198; Stuart, *Extracts from the Council Register*, 1:310; Clark, *Port of Aberdeen* 9, 16–17; Anderson, "Aberdonian Abroad," part 1, 42; and R. K. Hannay and Denys Hay, eds., *The Letters of James V Collected and Calendared* (Edinburgh: H. M. Stationery Office, 1954), 369.

Germany and Denmark were strongly affected by the new teaching,[5] so that the likeliest place from which the Reformed teachings came to Aberdeen was either Denmark or the Baltic.

5. W. Stanford Reid, "The Middle Class Factor in the Scottish Reformation," *Church History* 16 (1947), 145.

Appendix 2

Coping with Minister Shortages during the Early Reformation

The Reformers believed that the ministry of the Word and the administration of the sacraments should be in the hands of men set apart for that purpose. There was, however, a national shortage of qualified ministers in the early years of the Reformation. Within a generation or so this was to change, as educational standards were raised so that ministers who were nongraduates became rare.[1]

The Reformers envisaged three offices initially—ministers, exhorters, and readers—and that there could be a progression from reader to exhorter to minister. By the early 1570s, however, the office of exhorter died out, leaving ministers and readers. J. K. Cameron commented that the section "For Readers" in the First Book of Discipline "clearly reveals that the office is regarded as an expedient in the face of an emergency, and there is no indication that the office is expected to become a permanent feature of the ministry."[2] Nevertheless, readers played a key role in early years.

The shortage of ministers is clear from figures available for 1574. In that year there were, nationally, 289 ministers and 715 readers, with some parishes having both a minister and a reader. Readers, therefore, provided 70 percent of the pastoral care in those early Reformation years.[3] The work they did meant that they had a prominent role in parish life. They conducted a reader's service on Sundays

1. Donaldson, *Scotland: James V to VII*, 142.

2. J. K. Cameron, ed., *The First Book of Discipline* (Edinburgh: St. Andrew Press, 1972), 22.

3. Jane Dawson, "'The Word did everything': Readers, Singers and the Protes-

and on a weekday in towns. They were required to read chapters from the Bible and prayers from the psalm book, lead the congregation in prayer, and also take the lead as the congregation sang the metrical psalms.[4] In addition, the reader had the responsibility of officiating at rites of passage, which "made him the face of the new Reformed kirk for most of his parishioners."[5]

What all this meant was that congregation members, many of whom could not read or write, were constantly exposed to the Word of God: "The three skills that made each reader an invaluable asset to his parishioners were the ability to read, to write and to sing and they provided a bridge between the literate and non-literate worlds."[6]

This was the infant Reformed kirk's way of maintaining the importance of *sola Scriptura*, ensuring the congregations were under the sound of the Word of God, without the trappings that had gone before, until a more qualified ministry could be developed throughout the country.

---

tant Reformation in Scotland, c. 1560–1638," *Records of the Scottish Church History Society* 46 (2017): 6–7.

4. Dawson, "Word did everything," 13, 14, 18.

5. Dawson, "Word did everything," 27.

6. Dawson, "Word did everything," 36.

Glossary

Anabaptists. The name given to those who rejected infant baptism because they baptized again by immersion those who joined their communion on profession of faith in Christ.

Antinomians. The name given to those who rejected the moral law as not binding on Christians.

Arminianism. A theological system named after Jacob Arminius (Jakob Hermandszoon; 1560–1609), a Dutch theologian who taught, among other points, that Christ died for all people, that God's saving grace could be resisted, and that it was possible for Christians to fall from grace.

Brownism. A name often applied to independency, after Robert Brown (c. 1550–1633). He was a Puritan separatist who founded a number of Independent congregations in England.

Congregationalists. They held to a system of church government embracing two fundamental principles: (1) every local congregation of believers is a complete church, not subject to any ecclesiastical authority outside itself; and (2) all such local churches are in communion one with another and are bound to fulfill all the duties of such fellowship. The first principle made them distinct from presbyterianism, the second from independency.

Conventicles. A name given to the early assemblies of Wycliffe's followers. Later, it was given usually to the field preaching and "illegal" house services conducted by Scottish Presbyterian ministers ejected from their charges.

Engagement. The Engagement was a secret agreement between some Scottish nobles and the imprisoned Charles I by which the nobles undertook to raise an army to restore the king to the throne.

Episcopacy. Government by church officers called bishops.

Erastianism. From Thomas Erastus (1524–1583), Swiss theologian. This is the doctrine that the state has the right to intervene and overrule in church affairs.

Independents. The name given to certain bodies of Christians who assert that each Christian congregation is independent of all others and from all ecclesiastical authority except its own.

Infralapsarian (or **Sublapsarian**). The name given to those who consider the divine decree of election as dependent on that which permitted the introduction of evil. Hence, the decree occurred after the fall.

Prelacy. From the Latin *praeleti*, meaning "preferred or promoted above others." A state-supported episcopal system, an example being the Church of England.

Presbyterianism. A system of church government with a hierarchy of courts extending from the local kirk sessions through the presbytery and synod up to the national general assembly.

Puritans. Originally a term of abuse, it was applied to those who felt that the Reformation had not gone far enough. Noted for their zeal and fervor, Puritans placed great emphasis on spiritual experience and the need for conversion.

Supralapsarian. The name given to those who believed the decree of election, or predestination to eternal salvation or damnation, was the original decree on which all others depended. God intended to glorify His justice in the condemnation of some as well as His mercy in the salvation of others. Hence, the decree occurred before the fall.

Bibliography

Primary Sources

Aberdeen Council Letters. Edited by L. B. Taylor. Vols. 1–17. London: Oxford University Press, 1942–1950.

Anderson, P. J., ed. *Aberdeen Friars, Red, Black, White, Grey, Preliminary Calendar of Illustrative Documents*. Aberdeen: Aberdeen University Studies 40, 1909.

Baillie, Robert. The *Letters and Journals of Robert Baillie*. 3 vols. Edited by David Laing. Edinburgh: Bannatyne Club 73, 1841–1842.

Blakhal, Gilbert. *A Brieffe Narration of the Services Done to Three Noble Ladies*. Edited by John Stuart. Aberdeen: Spalding Club 2, 1844.

Burton, J. H., ed. *Register of the Privy Council of Scotland*. Series 1, vol. 1. Edinburgh, 1877.

Calderwood, David. *History of the Kirk of Scotland*. Edited by Thomas Thomson. 3 vols. Edinburgh: Wodrow Society, 1842–1849.

Calvin, John. *Commentary on the Book of Jeremiah and the Lamentations*. Vol. 1. Grand Rapids: Baker, 1981.

Cameron, J. K., ed. *The First Book of Discipline*. Edinburgh: St. Andrew Press, 1972.

Durham, James. *The Dying Man's Testament to the Church of Scotland, or A Treatise concerning Scandal*. Dallas, Tex.: Naphtali Press, 1990. First published 1659.

Fleming, Robert. *The Fulfilling of the Scripture*. Vol. 1. London: Forgotten Books, 2018. A reprint from Glasgow: Stephen Young, 1801.

Forbes-Leith, W., ed. *Historical Letters and Memoirs of Scottish Catholics, 1625–1793*. London: Longmans, Green, 1908.

———, ed. *Narrative of Scottish Catholics under Mary Stuart and James VI*. Edinburgh, 1885.

Gardiner, Samuel Rawson, ed. *Letters and Papers Illustrating the Relations between Charles II and Scotland in 1650*. Vol. 17 of Publications of the Scottish History Society. Edinburgh: Edinburgh University Press, 1894.

Gillies, John. *Historical Collections of Accounts of Revival*. Edinburgh: Banner of Truth, 1981. First published 1754; revised and enlarged 1845.

Gordon, James. *History of Scots Affairs from 1637 to 1641*. Edited by Joseph Robertson and George Grub. 3 vols. Aberdeen: Spalding Club 1–3, 1841.

Hannay, R. K., and Denys Hay, eds. *The Letters of James V Collected and Calendared*. Edinburgh: H. M. Stationery Office, 1954.

Johnston, Archibald. *Diary of Sir Archibald Johnston of Wariston*. Vol. 3, *1655–1660*. Scottish History Society 3, edited by James D. Ogilvie. Edinburgh: Edinburgh University Press and A. Constable Ltd., 1940.

Kistler, Don, ed. *The Puritans on Conversion*. Ligonier, Pa.: Soli Deo Gloria, 1990.

Knox, John. *History of the Reformation of Religion in Scotland*. Edited by W. C. Dickinson. 2 vols. London: Nelson, 1949.

Malthams, Walter J. *Rubies from Rutherford*. 2nd ed. Edinburgh: Oliphant Anderson and Ferrier, 1893.

Manuscript Records of the Kirk-Session of Aberdeen. CH2/448/1,2,3,4. National Archives, Edinburgh.

Melville, James. *The Diary of James Melville, 1556–1601*. Edited by G. R. Kinloch. Edinburgh: Bannatyne Club 34, 1829.

Mitchell, A. F. *Catechisms of the Second Reformation*. London: James Nisbet, 1886.

Peterkin, Alexander, ed. *Records of the Kirk of Scotland, Containing the Acts and Proceedings of the General Assemblies, from 1638 Downwards*. Edinburgh: John Sutherland, 1838.

Row, John. *The History of the Kirk of Scotland, from the Year 1558 to August 1637*. Edinburgh: Wodrow Society, 1842. With an appended continuation to July 1639 by his son John Row.

Rutherford, Samuel. *Catechism, or The Sum of Christian Religion*. Edinburgh: Blue Banner Productions, 1998.

———. *Christ Dying and Drawing Sinners to Himself*. Zeeland, Mich.: Reformed Church Publications, 2009.

———. *Conversations with a Dying Man*. Stornoway, Scotland: Reformation Press, 2017. First published in 1649 as *The Last and Heavenly Speeches, and Glorious Departure, of John Gordon, Viscount Kenmure*.

———. *The Covenant of Life Opened, or, A Treatise of the Covenant of Grace*. Edinburgh: Andrew Anderson, 1655.

———. *Fourteen Communion Sermons*. 2nd ed. Edinburgh: Blue Banner Productions, 1986. Originally published in Glasgow by Glass and Co., 1877.

———. *Influences of the Life of Grace*. London: Andrew Crook, 1658.

———. *Joshua Redivivus*. Edited by Robert McWard. 9th edition. Glasgow: John Bryce, 1765. This edition includes Samuel Rutherford's "Testimony to the Covenanted Work of Reformation (from 1638–1649), in Britain and Ireland." It includes also "Some of the Last Words of Mr. Rutherford; Containing Some Advices and Exhortations to His Friends and Relations, during His Sickness, before His Death."

———. *Lex, Rex or the Law and the Prince*. Harrisonburg, Va.: Sprinkle Publications, 1982.

———. *Letters of Samuel Rutherford*. Edited by Andrew A. Bonar. London: Oliphants, 1891.

———. *The Power of Faith and Prayer*. Stornoway: Reformation Press, 1991.

———. *Quaint Sermons Hitherto Unpublished*. Edited by A. A. Bonar. London: Hodder and Stoughton, 1885.

———. *The Trial and Triumph of Faith*. Edinburgh: William Collins, 1845.

Spalding, John. *Memorials of the Troubles in Scotland and England: A.D. 1624–A.D. 1645*. 2 vols. Aberdeen: Spalding Club 21, 23, 1850–51.

Stephen, James, ed. *Samuel Rutherford's Letters: Rearranged and Revised for Use of Modern Readers*. London: Pickering and Inglis, [1920?].

Stuart, John, ed. *Extracts from the Council Register of the Burgh of Aberdeen*. Vols. 1 and 2. Aberdeen: Spalding Club 12, 19, 1844–48.

Thomson, Thomas, ed. *Acts and Proceedings of the General Assemblies of the Kirk of Scotland*. 3 vols. Edinburgh: Bannatyne Club 81, 1839.

———, ed. *Acts of the Parliaments of Scotland*. Vols. 1–2. London, 1814.

Vogan, Matthew, ed. *"The King in His Beauty": The Piety of Samuel Rutherford*. Grand Rapids: Reformation Heritage Books, 2011.

Westminster Confession of Faith. Glasgow: Free Presbyterian Publications, 1973.

Secondary Sources

Anderson, Robert. "The Aberdonian Abroad," part 1. *Aberdeen University Review* 9, 1921–1922: 36–46.

Beeke, Joel, and Randall J. Pedersen. *Meet the Puritans*. Grand Rapids: Reformation Heritage Books, 2006.

Blaikie, W. G. *The Preachers of Scotland from the Sixth to the Nineteenth Century*. Edinburgh: Banner of Truth, 2001.

Brentnall, J. M. *Puritan and Covenanter Studies*. Swanick, Derbyshire, England: John M. Brentnall, n.d.

———. *Samuel Rutherford in Aberdeen*. Inverness, Scotland: John G. Eccles, 1981.

Burleigh, J. H. S. *A Church History of Scotland*. London: Oxford University Press, 1973.

Chambers, Robert. *Domestic Annals of Scotland, from the Reformation to the Rebellion of 1745*. Edinburgh: W. and R. Chambers, 1861.

Clark, V. E. *The Port of Aberdeen*. Aberdeen: D. Wylie and Son, 1921.

Coffey, John. *Politics, Religion, and the British Revolutions: The Mind of Samuel Rutherford*. Cambridge, England: Cambridge University Press, 1997.

Coffey, John, and Paul C. H. Lim, eds. *The Cambridge Companion to Puritanism*. Cambridge, England: Cambridge University Press, 2008.

Cook, Faith. *Grace in Winter: Rutherford in Verse*. Edinburgh: Banner of Truth, 1989.

———. *Samuel Rutherford and His Friends*. Edinburgh: Banner of Truth, 1992.

Crockett, S. R. *Raiderland: All about Grey Galloway*. London: Hodder and Stoughton, 1904.

Dawson, Jane. "'The Word did everything': Readers, Singers and the Protestant Reformation in Scotland, c.1560–1638." *Records of the Scottish Church History Society* 46 (2017): 1–37.

Dennison, E. Patricia, David Ditchburn, and Michael Lynch, eds. *Aberdeen before 1800: A New History*. East Linton, Scotland: Tuckwell Press, 2002.

DesBrisay, Gordon. "'The civill warrs did overrun all': Aberdeen, 1630–1690." In *Aberdeen before 1800: A New History*, edited by E. Patricia Dennison, David Ditchburn, and Michael Lynch, 238–66. East Linton, Scotland: Tuckwell Press, 2002.

Ditchburn, David. "Educating the Elite: Aberdeen and Its Universities." In *Aberdeen before 1800: A New History*, edited by E. Patricia Dennison, David Ditchburn, and Michael Lynch, 327–46. East Linton, Scotland: Tuckwell Press, 2002.

Donaldson, Gordon. "The Galloway Clergy at the Reformation." *Dumfriesshire and Galloway Natural History and Antiquarian Society Transactions* 30, ser. 3 (1951–52): 38–60.

———. *The Making of the Scottish Prayer Book of 1637*. Edinburgh: Edinburgh University Press, 1954.

———. *Scotland: James V to James VII*. Edinburgh: Oliver and Boyd, 1965.

Ferrie, Hugh. "Some Pre-Reformation Scots in Denmark." *Innes Review* 3 (1952): 130–31.

Fleming, D. Hay. *The Story of the Scottish Covenants*. Edinburgh: Oliphant, Anderson and Ferrier, 1904.

Fleming, J. A. *Flemish Influence in Britain*. Vol. 1. Glasgow: Jackson, Wylie, 1930.

Gilmour, Robert. *Samuel Rutherford: A Study Biographical and Somewhat Critical, in the History of the Scottish Covenant*. Edinburgh: Oliphant, Anderson and Ferrier, 1904.

Haws, C. H. "The Diocese of Aberdeen and the Reformation." *Innes Review* 22, no. 2 (1972): 72–84.

Henderson, G. D. *The Burning Bush*. Edinburgh: Saint Andrew Press, 1957.

———. *Religious Life in Seventeenth Century Scotland*. Cambridge: Cambridge University Press, 1937.

Hewison, J. King. *The Covenanters*. Vol. 1. Glasgow: John Smith and Son, 1908.

Horne, A. Sinclair. *Torchbearers of the Truth: Sketches of the Scottish Covenanters*. Edinburgh: Scottish Reformation Society, 1968.

Howie, John. *The Scots Worthies*. Revised by W. H. Carslaw. Edinburgh: Oliphant, Anderson and Ferrier, 1870.

Innes, A. Taylor. *Studies in Scottish History, Chiefly Ecclesiastical*. London: Hodder and Stoughton, 1892.

Isbell, Sherman. "Introduction to Samuel Rutherford's 'The Due Right of Presbyteries.'" In *Samuel Rutherford: An Introduction to His Theology*, edited by Matthew Vogan, 213–28. Academic Series. Edinburgh: Scottish Reformation Society, 2012.

Keddie, John. "George Gillespie and the Westminster Assembly." *Scottish Reformation Society Historical Journal* 8 (2018): 44–57.

Kennedy, William. *Annals of Aberdeen*. Vol. 2. London, 1818.

Kerr, James. *The Covenants and the Covenanters*. Edinburgh: R. W. Hunter, 1895.

Kirk, James. *Patterns of Reform: Continuity and Change in the Reformation Kirk*. Edinburgh: T&T Clark, 1989.

Loane, Marcus L. *Makers of Religious Freedom: Henderson, Rutherford, Bunyan, Baxter*. London: Inter-Varsity, 1960.

Lynch, Michael, Gordon DesBrisay, with Murray G. H. Pittock. "The Faith of the People." In *Aberdeen before 1800: A New History*, edited by E. Patricia Dennison, David Ditchburn, and Michael Lynch, 327–46. East Linton, Scotland: Tuckwell Press, 2002.

Macleod, John. *Scottish Theology in Relation to Church History*. Edinburgh: Banner of Truth, 2015.

McCrie, Thomas. *Lives of Alexander Henderson and James Guthrie, with Specimens of Their Writings*. Edinburgh: John Greig, 1846.

———. *Sketches of Scottish Church History: Embracing the Period from the Reformation to the Revolution*. Edinburgh: John Johnstone, 1841.

McLennan, Bruce. "Presbyterianism Challenged: A Study of Catholicism and Episcopacy in the North-East of Scotland, 1560–1650." PhD thesis, Aberdeen University, 1977.

McMillan, Catherine. "'Scho refuseit altogidder to heir his voce': Women and Catholic Recusancy in North East Scotland, 1560–1610." *Records of the Scottish Church History Society* 45 (2016): 38–48.

Morton, Alexander S. *Galloway and the Covenanters; or, The Struggle for Religious Liberty in the South-West of Scotland*. Paisley, Scotland: Alexander Gardner, 1914.

Murray, Thomas. *The Life of Samuel Rutherford*. Edinburgh: Oliphant and Sons, 1828.

Reid, W. Stanford. "The Middle Class Factor in the Scottish Reformation." *Church History* 16 (1947): 137–53.

Rendell, Kingsley G. *Samuel Rutherford: A New Biography of the Man and His Ministry*. Fearn, Ross-shire, Scotland: Christian Focus, 2003.

Richard, Guy M. *The Supremacy of God in the Theology of Samuel Rutherford*. Milton Keynes, England: Paternoster, 2008.

———. "The Two Shall Become One Flesh: Samuel Rutherford's 'Affectionate' Theology of Union with Christ in the Song of Songs." In *Samuel Rutherford: An Introduction to His Theology*, edited by Matthew Vogan, 77–110. Academic Series. Edinburgh: Scottish Reformation Society, 2012.

Roberts, Maurice. "Samuel Rutherford: 'The Comings and Goings of the Heavenly Bridegroom.'" In *The Trials of Puritanism*, by Samuel T. Logan Jr. et al., 119–34. Westminster Conference Papers, 1993. Mirfield: Westminster Conference Secretary, [1994]. Presented as a paper at the 1993 Westminster Conference.

Ross, J. M. "The Salient Features of Rutherford's Spirituality." *The Month, A Review of Christian Thought and World Affairs* (July1975).

Sanderson, M. H. B. *Ayrshire and the Reformation: People and Change*. East Linton, Scotland: Tuckwell Press, 1997.

Smellie, Alexander. *Men of the Covenant*. Edinburgh: Banner of Truth, 1975.

Somerset, Douglas. "The 'Alteration of Religion' in Aberdeen in 1559: An Ancient and Persistent Historical Error." *Scottish Reformation Society Historical Journal* 4 (2014): 1–62.

Stephen, Jeffrey. "The Not So Conservative North: Covenanting Strength in 1638–39." *Scottish Reformation Society Historical Journal* 5 (2015): 63–81.

Stephen, Thomas. *The History of the Church of Scotland, from the Reformation to the Present Time*. Vols. 1 and 2. London: Simpkin, Marshall, 1844.

Stewart, David. "The 'Aberdeen Doctors' and the Covenanters." *Records of the Scottish Church History Society* 22 (1984): 35–44.

Thomson, Andrew. *Samuel Rutherford*. London: Hodder and Stoughton, 1884.

Todd, Margo. *The Culture of Protestantism in Early Modern Scotland*. New Haven, Conn.: Yale University Press, 2002.

Tweedie, W. K., ed. *Scottish Puritans: Select Biographies*. 2 vols. Edinburgh: Banner of Truth, 2008.

Vogan, Matthew, ed. *Samuel Rutherford: An Introduction to His Theology*. Academic Series. Edinburgh: Scottish Reformation Society, 2012.

———. "Samuel Rutherford's Experience and Doctrine of Conversion." *Scottish Reformation Society Historical Journal* 5 (2015): 35–62.

Vos, Johannes G. *The Scottish Covenanters: Their Origins, History and Distinctive Doctrines*. Kilsyth, Scotland: Blue Banner Productions, 2018.

Walker, James. *The Theology and Theologians of Scotland Chiefly of the Seventeenth and Eighteenth Centuries*. Edinburgh: T&T Clark, 1888.

Watt, William. *A History of Aberdeen and Banff*. County History Series. Edinburgh: William Blackwell, 1900.

Whyte, Alexander. *Samuel Rutherford and Some of His Correspondents*. Edinburgh: Oliphant, Anderson and Ferrier, 1894.